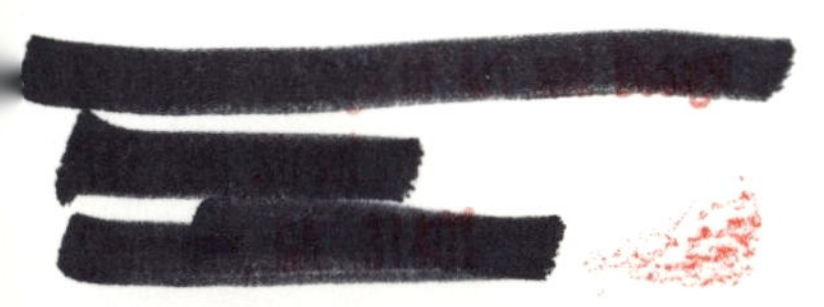

THE
TEACHER OF CHINA PAINTING

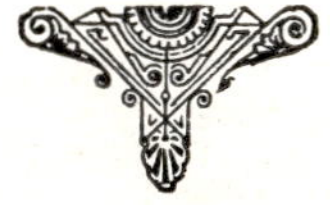

BY

D. M. CAMPANA

10th Reprint

IMPORTANT NOTICE.

In compiling this book, our first aim was to write a useful text for serious workers, giving our method of producing good work, and the fruit of a long and practical experience. We thought, by gathering the matter concerning the painting of porcelain and explaining the different processes in a short and practical manner, to make the book of valuable help to students of this branch of painting.

Any historic data of the invention of porcelain, the various styles of decoration, or its discoverers, we thought best to omit, believing that such matter is to be found in books especially devoted to the historical side of china painting.

It was deemed necessary, however, to give the rudiments for the benefit of beginners, as well as sound advice for more advanced workers.

The fruit of twenty years' experience will, we hope, help to explain and to prevent many of the unpleasant surprises so apt to come in the decorating and firing of porcelain.

In short, we hope to have succeeded in producing a practical manual to meet all the requirements for the student of this branch of art, and may our success in our demonstrations, and our help to someone to whom our opportunities in this rather mysterious field were not granted, be proportionate to the honesty and sincerity of our intentions.

D. M. CAMPANA.

PREFACE

Students should always refer to index for any advice pertaining to rules, materials, incidents, recipes, methods, etc., as all matter belonging to special branches has been carefully gathered in separate chapters, clearly named and listed in the index at the end of this book. General matters concerning ground-laying, for instance, giving method, oils, mistakes, colors, etc., are found in chapter called *Ground-laying;* hints or directions pertaining to firing, such as stacking of the china, materials for the kiln, accident of cracking, smoothing off rough china, etc., will be found collected under the chapter, *Firing Suggestions,* and by referring to different chapters, as circumstances may arise, students will be able to find valuable help, and good advice in any case, as this book contains everything worth knowing in the china decorating, up to this time. The writer has very often received inquiries from students on matters well explained in this book (which book they already had at hand), which showed they had not properly read it. An occasional rereading, from beginning to end, will be very beneficial to students, and will refresh their memory as to many useful subjects therein included.

If students are completely *new* to the decorating of china, they should refer at first to chapter *Mixing of China Colors,* specially written for them; should carefully peruse the subject and, above all, should be patient in the following of all rules. To learn an art without teacher, and from text-book, is a very difficult task, but if students are impatient and want everything done without effort, and think success should come their way, the learning of such art will be still more difficult. China painting, technically, is not very difficult, but in learning without a teacher to start you off, you may, for instance, use too thick a color, or color badly ground, or too much oil, or not wash your brush sufficiently well. In the first instance, thick colors will chip off. Badly ground colors will look rough and gritty. Too much oil will cause colors to run, or will blister in the firing. If so, do better on second trial. It costs time and money, but you can not pretend to learn a valuable profession without work and expenses. Also do not put the blame on your book, as the book cannot draw your hand, or slap your wrist when you make mistakes. If you can take a lesson or two, to have a fair idea of the work, do so by all means, but if you cannot, exploit this textbook; **read it**; study it, and you will find it complete.

CHAPTER 1
CONVENTIONAL DESIGNING

A student in art work must compare. The individual opinion of a few persons is of no value whatever in the field of art; until students have seen productions in large numbers, and of different styles, and in comparing their values have discovered the point of beauty and the possibilities in the future of this art.

Therefore, artists and craftsmen have agreed upon certain fundamental principles, deducted mostly from the best types of ancient ornament, and from the observation of nature applied to good decorations. These fundamental principles may be classified as follows: Balance, Contrast of Spacing, Subordination, Symmetry, Unity, Repose. Ornament in general, may be divided into two classes: 1. Geometrical, including forms like triangles, circles, zigzag, or any other form based on geometry, having no suggestion of nature, and whose beauty is derived chiefly from the harmonious contrast and intersection of lines and forms. 2. Designs made to represent or to suggest natural subjects, such as plants, animals, figures, etc., though not to be perfect likenesses, necessarily.

The modern commercial spirit has had a very marked influence upon the recent styles of decoration and has partly done away with much of the tedious work that geometrical designs required, in this manner giving a strong impulse to a style of work, usually called conventional decoration, but which we might properly call a scientific application of natural forms and color. Owen Jones, in his "Grammar of Ornament," states as a fundamental principle that "The decorative arts arise from, and should properly be attendant upon archi-

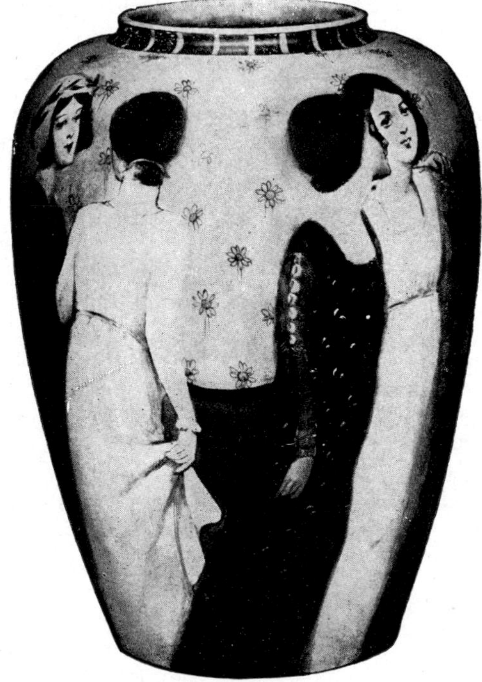

Figure No. 1

tecture," and, keeping this in mind, we will adapt this rule to the decoration of china, with reference to shape.

The decoration of a vase should depend upon the form of the vase itself; the purpose being solely to improve the appearance of the shape, rather than the display of a decorative motif. Art demands that different objects serve different purposes in decoration; the function of oil painting is to tell a story; that of furniture, to offer comfort; of drapery, to cover walls; of curtains, to subdue the light.

And pottery has also its mission; not a mission of individual contrasts, or representation of subjects, but of co-operating in producing a harmonious effect in the decorating of a room in a whole, to soften or to enliven, to reduce the emptiness of a corner, or break an unpleasant line on a mantel piece. In other words, we must have a fitness of purpose in everything.

The decoration will have the same relation to the vase that the vase bears to the room, its mission being to enhance the shape, with the aid of properly balanced lines and subdued colors, suggestive either of natural or purely geometrical subjects.

Considering the large number of forms introduced into the market, it would be a difficult matter to give a rule for decorations complying with the different shapes, even if our space were unlimited. We will only attempt to call attention to certain forms and conditions which should always influence the decorative designer of china painting. Consider first the shape to be decorated and see which form of decoration would be most appropriate. Does the vase suggest Grecian, Roman, Renaissance, or Colonial modeling? Decorations that would comply perfectly with the style of shape should be applied, be it Roman or Grecian, Colonial, etc.

If the vase has a more liberal form, a straight cylinder or a squatty bowl, a modern tea set, or a stein, suggesting the modern style of modeling, apply a more liberal design, give vent to your own ideas, which may cover a much larger field, and compose a design subordinate to the shape.

A student came to us one day and brought specimens of her work to show us how far her education had come. A Colonial coffee set was decorated with Chinese dragons and designs. A recent make of punch bowl was decorated in fruit with scroll of rococo ornaments; and a 15th century figure panel was surrounded by art *nouveau* suggestions and other incongruous mixtures of styles which practically spoiled the artistic value of her works.

This should be absolutely avoided, and one style kept in every particular part of the whole. Having called the attention to the necessity of selecting the proper decoration, we will warn the student to use good judgment in choosing good shapes of china. A badly proportioned vase with a broad top, small feet, adorned with useless scrolls and ornaments, with an elaborate and badly proportioned handle and bad lines, will always, even if correctly decorated, be a useless and inartistic vase. Always select a sober form, made to fill its life purpose, without affected ornamentations; one with simple lines and good proportions.

As we said before, it would be difficult to explain in writing, or to lay down any law for the application of decorations, without leading the student to a rigid adherence to a fixed formula, which is to be avoided. In art, the last word is never said, and various decorations made by different artists, may be the exponents of ideas that are different, but equally good.

The foundation of good decoration is the harmony of lines and colors and the disposition of these so as best to produce a well balanced contrast. A vase, or any other shape that is meant to decorate a room, will be seen from various points of view, and should be so decorated that the subject, no matter from where it is seen, will always convey its full meaning. A printed notice, pasted around a telegraph pole, will compel the reader to walk around it in order to grasp its content. This example clearly explains the value of rhythmical design, which, even if not necessarily perfect in regard to symmetry, will occupy a limited space and succeed itself around the vase, in this manner giving to the observer a certain suggestion of forward movement. A forward movement is obtained by an intersection of lines, slightly bent toward a special direction, either connected or disconnected, but applied so that one will succeed the other. A person standing perfectly erect, suggests stability, while a person in motion will take a somewhat oblique line, head forward, and the more rapid the movement of the person the more oblique will be the line. This may be applied to the disposition of any decoration whose theme of lines may convey a forward motion; these designs are very appropriate for perfectly round shapes. A border of symmetrical design will suggest unity and movement, and if applied in the right place, will always be helpful to a round form.   An upward movement is suggested by breadth at the lower part of a design in proportion to the narrowness at the top.   A bottle-shaped vase placed head downward, would always look incongruous,

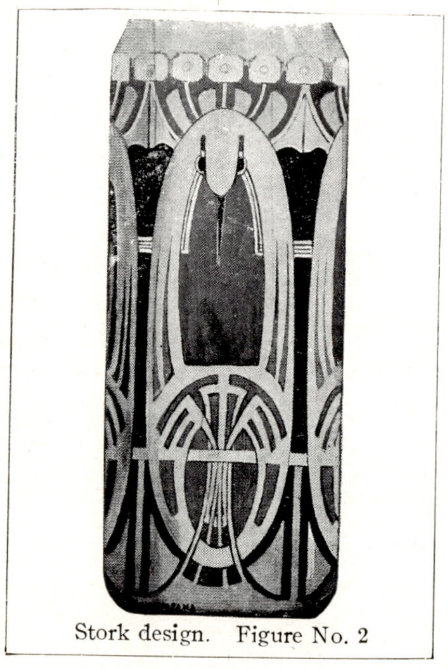

Stork design.   Figure No. 2

and not only would the weight at the top offend the artistic eye, but it would also be highly impracticable. The same vase in its correct position, broad at the base and graceful at the neck, will express a feeling of upward motion, which, being in accordance with the natural laws of gravity, is also taken as a fundamental law in the field of decorative art. The decoration of pottery and china, therefore, should generally be heavier at the base, and lighter at the top, in order to assist the shape of the vase in representing its proper upward movement, just as the forward movement suggests the rounding motion, which assists a vase so materially in bringing out its own roundness. Upon the intersection of these two movements, with the addition of the horizontal lines, which we will call the running movement, is based the whole composition of any design in pottery. For the present, let us keep to articles like vases, jars, etc., of round shape. After having selected a subject to be painted on the china, your first aim should be to divide and subdivide it so that the whole will produce a well balanced contrast of spaces. The subject may be placed on the high part of the vase, either in sections or connectedly, producing either a border, a panel, or a scroll, etc. It may also be placed at the center or on the high part of the vase, as shown in figures 5 and 7.

In figure 7, we use the upward movement almost entirely, and the subject, a symmetrical landscape, conveys, of itself, the same expression of line. Figure 2 is an example of the intersection of curved lines. It will be observed that in any one of these examples, the usefulness of the forward movement is demonstrated; in figure 7, by the succession of the perspective, and in figure 5, in the successive connection of the central motif. It will also be observed that the principal mass of color is placed so as to accentuate the solidity of the lower part of the vase. It is quite necessary to avoid, if possible, any strong line which would suggest the division of the vase into two equal parts. In figure 7, the design is above the middle of the vase; and in figure 5, it occupies fully three-quarters of the space. In the application of design, always remember to dispose your subject so as to afford a rational contrast of spacing and to convey the feelings of balance and repose. If large spaces and shadows are associated with unusually small ones, the eye will not be able to discern any relation between their various areas, and this would violate the first principle of balance. The good taste and judgment which come from the careful observation of good examples, are the safest guides and helps for obtaining well balanced contrasts, as no rule would answer for all the varied shapes of pottery. For instance, to balance a certain mass of color placed on one side, another quantity (according to size and position) should be put above or below the former mass. It is necessary to know that a certain space of white has also its weight in the producing of balance; and as we see on figure 11, the broad, low white space, in connection with the little black square below, counter-balances the heavier spots of the top. Of course, in ceramics the value of different colors will come to the assistance of the artist, and a large but light design on the top of the vase, apparently against the fundamental principle of designing, can easily be balanced by a line at the bottom, if such a line be of sufficient strength. The grays, blacks, violets, and all neutral tints we will call heavy colors; while the yellows, reds, light greens, etc., can be called light, and by a combination of colors and spaces a proper balance of the china will be attained.

After planning the composition of the design, plan the color scheme, and it would be helpful to work out the design in water colors first. This will save time, will permit the making of certain changes, and, above all, will offer an adequate idea of the balance of the design. Figure 4 will give an idea of spacing, well balanced, and of good relation between light and shadow. In figure 3 the subject lacks unity. The swans are disconnected, making a bad border. The lilies under the border are unnecessary, detracting the attention from the main subject, giving the whole decoration a lack of subordination.

In figure 4, the design appears more adequate and restful. The lower part of the bowl conveys the idea of solidity; the border is well connected and subdued. The subject, or motif, shows rather faintly, but still sufficiently well to be thoroughly understood. It is a composition that is well balanced with the shape and size of the china. It may be seen from this very limited demonstration, that the *first* requirement is to adapt the size of the subject to the size of the pottery and to reduce any contrast of colors that may interfere in producing balance of spacing, and repose. Secondly, avoid any disconnection of the forward movement, so as to preserve the unity of the design. Thirdly, it is necessary to have the subject clearly understood, though not neces sarily prominent, in order to keep the suggestiveness of the motif, and not lose track of it.

A few plates will be devoted to illustrations of table ware. Figure 8 represents a plate decorated with grapes symmetrically disposed, so as to form a border. It will be seen that the design is divided into four equal

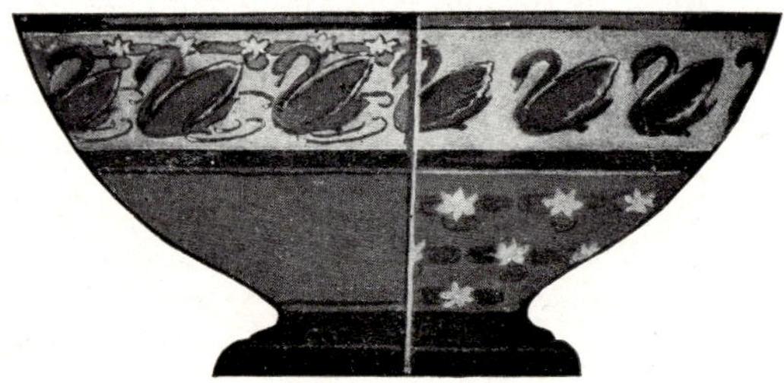

Figure 3   Figure 4

parts, thus giving the impression of cross lines, and of a square, which, in a flat circular form, is not desirable; moreover, the grapes are too literally taken from nature. In figure 6, we attempt to solve the same problem in tulips for plate decoration, but in a more appropriate way. Figure 10 is a design for a game plate with pheasants for a motif. In this design, the movement of the subject, which conveys the idea of roundness, is satisfying. The leaning pheasant alone would make a disconnected line, while with the addition of the second, there seems to be a better subordination of design and unity of curve.

The important principle, which must not be forgotten, is that the different parts composing the design should have something in common, and should share the same property. For instance, it would be absurd to add to the plates, figures 6, 8, 10, any design suggesting Colonial, Renaissance, or any other style of ornament, or to bring in flowers or leaves. Be very careful not to bring together any contrasting ideas. This is not only to preserve the character of the decoration, but also to avoid pictorial suggestions, which were never intended for table ware. Decorations, as was stated at the head of this chapter, are only to embellish the china not to tell a story. Let the imagination find the solution or work out the suggestions, and at the same time enjoy the delicacy and harmony of line and color.

A serious designer, who really tries to improve and to produce artistic decorations, will soon discover that his field of expression in china is not that of the painter or illustrator, and that his ideas must conform to certain mathematical principles. Thus far we have only spoken of decorations suggested by natural forms, which, from a commercial standpoint, may be more practical, as they are made more quickly; but we still wish to convince the student of the fact that, geometrical decorations are equally good, and really perhaps more decorative.

Certainly nothing could be more beautiful than the Greek and Roman frets; and a good scroll, which harmonizes so well with any simple shape, makes a beautiful decoration.

In conclusion, let us sum up the different principles

already spoken of, which should always be good references for the production of appropriate decorations.

1. Select a good form to be decorated.

2. Apply a design that is in keeping with the style of the shape.

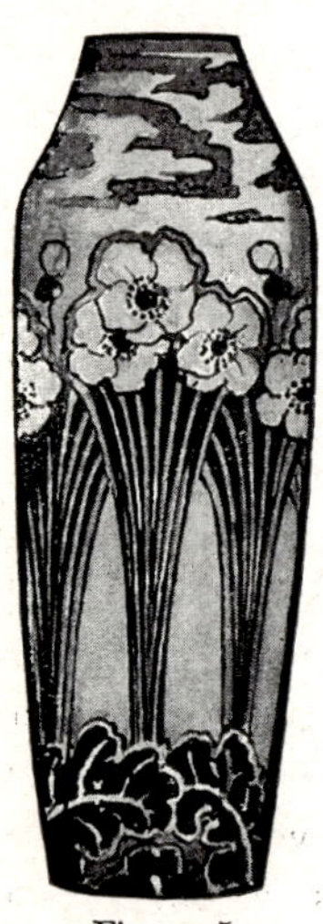

Figure 5

3. Use the same subject (though perhaps treated a little differently) for the various details of your work. If the decoration be some prescribed ornament, be careful to keep to the pure style of this ornament.

4. Remember that it is one of the fundamental laws of balance, that the lower part of a vase., should appear more solid than the top.

5. Dispose your decorative subject in such a way that it will be understood, no matter from which point of view it is seen.

6. Avoid overcrowding, and do not have too large a design. Be reminded of the necessity of dividing the subject well so as to produce a well balanced decoration.

7. Keep the design simple, and avoid any striking contrast in color, as this fault would detract the attention from the shape of the vase.

8. Connect the different designs, so that they will not appear to be isolated or suspended in the air.

9. Do not keep to nature too closely. Use nature,

merely as an inspiration for good forms and lines.

10. Use correct movement. If the shape be tall and straight, let the lines of decoration be tall, vertical, or slightly inclined or broken in such a way as to fulfil the requirements of upward movement. If the form is convex, let the lines of decorations express forward movement. A long vertical line will look badly on a convex shape.

11. Avoid all glaring contrasts; do not make use of gold, silver, bronze, etc., on china. Pure art will not permit deception, and the use of metals or jewels, on earthen ware, would come under the head of inappropriate counterfeits.

12. Do not apply your decorations so as to divide your china in the center. This is not good taste.

These rules are always adhered to by connoisseurs of decorative articles and by juries of art exhibitions. In following these principles, the student will be going in the right direction and will soon be able to produce artistic work.

Of course, flat plaques, tiles, and slabs can be painted in a more naturalistic manner, but for the fitness of things let us apply to them also a decorative purpose different from the oil and water color painting. Cut No. 9 is a reproduction of a plaque with decorative application of trees and figure. The movement of the trees suggests the circular movement adhering to the round plaque; the figure in the center, in flat tint, is also stooping over in a natural manner, and its light color imparts a feeling of center to the whole. In demanding that china decorations be suggestive only, we are expressing the views of the craft workers in general —those who design draperies, metal work, or pottery, whose special aim is to stimulate the imagination to unravel the decorated suggestions. It has often been held that when art will reproduce nature literally, this will be the symptoms of the lack of imagination and idealization, which are forerunners of the decadence of art.

CHAPTER II
SUGGESTIONS FOR FIRING CHINA

Do you remember how proud you were in contemplating the first china you fired successfully? Since then you have under-fired and over-fired your decorations many times, and you will agree with us that there is always much anxiety during the firing of your best work. We saw recently how an expert, doing nothing but firing for the last 20 years, had reduced a round glass globe to a flat cake shape, and insisted that he had given all possible attention to his work.

We therefore warn the student not to feel overconfident and to remember the following fundamental rules for the firing of china.

If possible, have your kiln in a dry place; otherwise, you must dry the kiln with a short fire before stacking it. If the elementary rules are followed, there will be nothing dangerous about kilns, no matter where they are placed. To insure a free and reliable draught, have a long chimney that has free access to plenty of air; not one opening into a narrow court for instance, nor one so close to other buildings that the draught might be interfered with. If it is necessary to connect the kiln pipe with the chimney of the house, be sure that the draught is strong enough to produce a good roaring sound. Never let the oil overflow. If it does, and burns, turn off the oil and let the fire go out naturally; then start again. There is no danger of spoiling the china. To prevent any trouble of fires it will be well to have a broad tin pan under the burner.

There is no specified time for firing, but if the weather is stormy or very warm, a much longer time will be required to produce the necessary heat. Air bubbles are apt to stop the flow of the oil. A small wire will remedy this easily enough. Should the fire go out, however, let it cool before beginning again. Keep the oil can open on top, so that the oil may flow more freely. Kilns, especially those with iron pots, should be whitewashed, periodically, to insure a better glaze.

All manufacturers furnish complete instructions for the mounting of their kilns. They should be kept in good repair, and all cracks should be carefully plastered up with kiln clay. This is especially true of gas kilns, as, if only a small quantity of gas should escape into the pot, all the colors will turn to a muddy gray. Keep the kiln free from dust by rubbing it with a stiff, dry brush after every firing. Place the shelves (provided you are going to use them) before placing any china. See that the pieces stand firmly and solidly. French china should be placed in the back of the kiln. We call the front of the kiln the side toward the door, and the

back of the kiln the opposite closed side. The back and
lower parts receive the strongest fire; the front and
higher parts, the lighter. Two pieces coming in contact with each other will not stick if one of them is
unglazed, but they will if both are glazed. This does

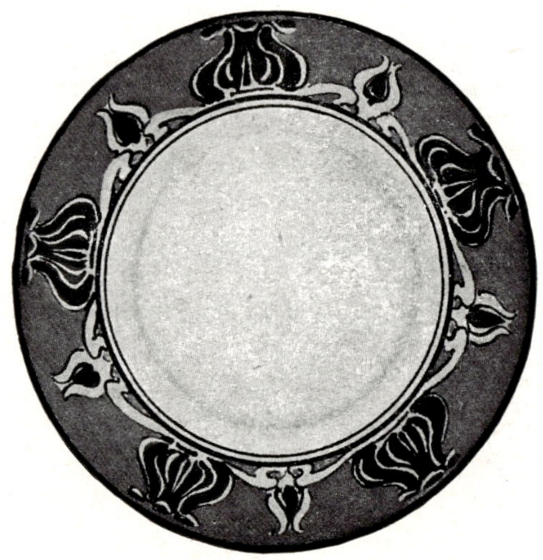

Figure 6

not apply to soft ware like Belleek, English china, etc.,
which is so soft, that contact in the kiln is always dangerous. Do not put heavy articles inside of bowls or
other concave pieces, as they are apt to collapse under
the influence of the heat. Stack plates, cups, etc., with
stilts or asbestos, so that they may not stick together.
Pieces of thick asbestos cord are very serviceable for

stacking. Asbestos boards are used under china and sometimes between china and walls, to prevent cracking. An asbestos cord may be tied around a broken piece to keep it together. Of course, the broken china must be cemented first. The asbestos will leave no mark on white French china, and, if the fire is light, will leave none over the decorated parts. Asbestos leaves no marks over gold, but will show on Belleek or English ware.

To prevent the cracking of Belleek ware, place it upon bricks and on asbestos; this is to allow a slow and even heating. Cracking is caused by the uneven expansion of the china. The bottom of vases is generally heavier than the top, and the thinner part, expanding quicker than the other when the heat becomes effective, the cracking follows. Many Belleek pieces have also been broken by drying them too quickly over artificial heat. To prevent cracking in the kiln, place these pieces either head downward, or else as far as possible above the bottom of the kiln, and be careful to fire very slowly. Iron kilns are the most successful in firing Belleek china and soft tiles safely, because their heat is more evenly distributed. If Belleek pieces are placed head downwards on asbestos cords, a slight mark will be left on the edges, which can be very easily smoothed off. If the edge is covered with gold, such asbestos will leave no mark at all.

Do not decorate china that has already been used at table, as the glazes are affected by the greasy substances already absorbed, and the result will be very unsatisfactory. It is safer, though not necessary, to dry the china before firing, to prevent the dust from sticking to the fresh colors. Always remember to allow a small draught under the bottom of every china piece; this is for safety.

Stack plates, one over the other, supported by stilts or asbestos, and see that the stack is straight and steady. They may also be fired standing on edge or on top of certain pieces. As we said before, with the exception of Belleek ware, an unglazed edge put next to a glazed surface will not stick to it.

Grays, blues, and pinks stand the strongest firing; then come the greens, and the yellows, then the browns, and the purples, and least and last, the reds and the flesh tones. Gold will stand a medium fire, will rub off if under-fired, and will look weak if over-fired.

Liquid bright gold and silver require a medium fire. Keep soft ware in the front of the kiln. Leave sufficient room between pieces, so that even when they expand they will not touch.

We do not agree on the strong firing generally advised for lustre colors. Give your lustres a Belleek firing, and these over gold, should be especially lightly fired. Glass requires a much lighter firing than china.

Now, if everything is in order, close the door of the kiln gently and let the oil into the burner. Allow about ten minutes for the little asbestos fibers to become saturated, before applying the match. The preliminary work of the lighting and drying out of the kiln could really be done while stacking the china, so as to save time. The oil having run drop by drop for about 15 minutes, let it flow now a little more freely for about one-half hour, and then give it still a better flow. The last fifteen minutes of firing should be generously strong, in order to bring out the glaze quickly. The same sort of a rule will apply to a gas kiln. From two to three hours is the usual time for firing. The lower part of the kiln will begin to show a dark red color, gradually becoming brighter after about an hour and a

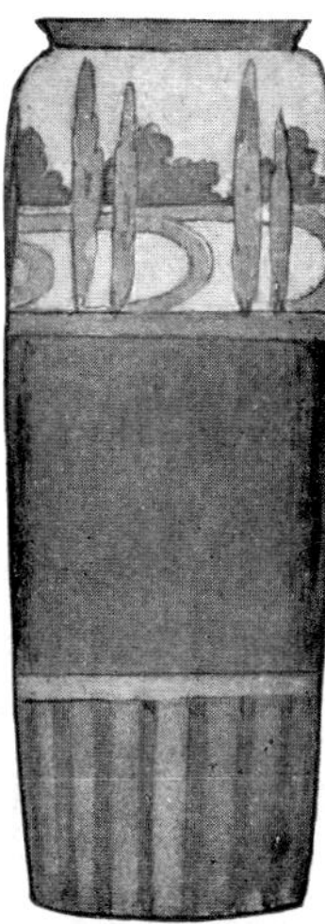

Figure No. 7

half. When it has reached a whitish red shade, turn off the oil. When the day is stormy and dark, the red inside the kiln will appear brighter than it really is, and possibly deceive you in closing the fire too soon. Many artists shut off the fire when the pieces show a glossy, even appearance, which they say is the required glaze. There are also little melting tests which are placed in front of the spy hole, which tests in melting will show the degree of heat. Study well the peculiarities of your kiln. A damper on the chimney will regulate its cooling, and also the draught.

The chimney should be cleaned every six months or so, as the soot may prevent a good draught and might set the chimney on fire. Should this happen, turn off the oil, and let the soot consume itself with its own fire. This will not hurt the china in the least. Too much smoke from the chimney is a sign of an unnecessary waste of oil.

About three or four hours should be allowed for cooling, and in opening the door be careful not to subject the china to a sudden cool draught. Open the door only very gradually, leaving a mere crack at first, then a little larger space, etc. The sudden draught of cool air might cause the china to craze and crack.

A piece of soft glazed ware, if taken from the kiln while still too warm, is apt to show a crackled or crazed glaze, and you will hear the little crackling sound produced by the sudden contraction of the glaze.

Much care should be taken in cooling off a kiln filled with china, for fear of having the china broken. The case is entirely different with the firing of glass. In this latter, it is strongly advised to open the door of the kiln right after the oil is turned off. This early opening will not only produce a better gloss on the glass, but will also prevent the after-heating, which is liable to melt the glass. This task will seem a very difficult matter for an amateur, but it should be understood that the door of the kiln may be open only one or two inches.

Note.—See list of prices for firing—page 135.

CHAPTER III
LUSTRE COLORS

If you like to lose your temper, use lustre colors. This is certainly the best recipe for it, as you very seldom can reproduce a good lustre piece just as you like it and a color producing a certain tint this time, will give different effect later—perhaps better, perhaps not so good, but different. Still, lustre painting is fascinating and interesting, and very charming things, especially small sized articles, are accomplished with these colors. The lighter tints are more reliable than the darker ones, as a rule.

Lustres are bought in liquid form, and before firing they all look very much alike. Keep the bottles closed, and do not use the cork of one bottle for another. They are to be applied with as large a square shader as possible, and the fewer the strokes, the smoother will be the effect.

The brushes must be perfectly clean. Use turpentine first and then alcohol, to clean them; and dry them thoroughly before using. It would be desirable, though not absolutely necessary, to have a separate brush for each lustre. Under no circumstances should turpentine come in contact with them. If it is necessary to use a thinner, take oil of lavender or essence for thinning. To rub off unfired lustres, use alcohol. To outline a design over or under unfired lustres, the outlining china colors should be mixed with water and a very little syrup of sugar or mucilage, but no turpentine. (See the chapter on Outlining.) If under the lustres, dry the outline well before applying the liquid; if over, the lustre should be thoroughly dry before applying the outlines. Ink or pencil outline left under lustre will show badly and will affect the colors.

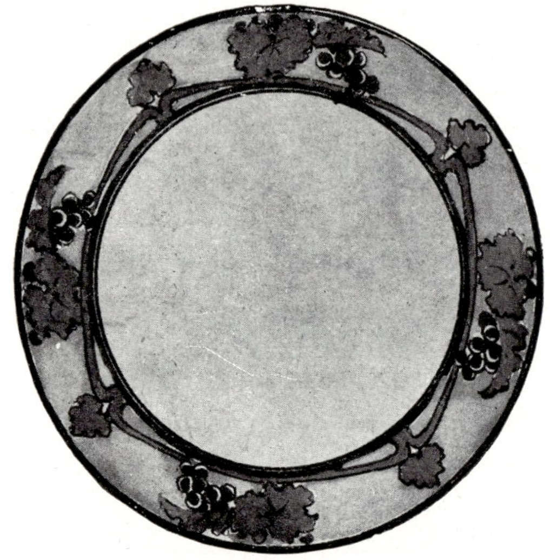

Figure No. 8

These colors can be used on crystal glass as well as on china, but the results are apt to be more uncertain. They require belleek or medium firing, but will rub off if fired too lightly. French china as well as Belleek will give satisfactory results.

The different pearls, viz., opal, mother of pearl, yellow pearl, green pearl, and iridescent, require a more generous firing than the greens, yellows, blues, etc. Over fired lustres use Roman gold.

In handling a lustre tinted piece, remember that finger marks will show. Before applying them, clean the china thoroughly, perhaps even using alcohol. Blemishes and spots on fired lustres are caused by dust on the brush, on the china, or in the kiln, by dampness, by turpentine, or by handling. After they are applied, therefore, dry them well by artificial heat, and wrap the pieces in thin paper, using no cotton for this purpose, as cotton will stick and cause blemishes.

Fire the china as soon as possible, or at least, keep it in a dry place. It will be safest to apply the lustre in the last firing, as an extra firing might possibly mar their beauty, unless they are reapplied each time. To produce even tints, repeat the lustres for several firings, but do not attempt to apply an extra coat of it over an unfired one, as the unfired lustre would soften and expand, and the result would be a blotched effect.

An unsatisfactory, spotted lustre can be corrected by reapplying the same color, or by covering it with a darker tint; also by covering the faulty part with a generous coat of mother of pearl. If the lustre comes out of the firing too light, reapply same and refire.

The padding of lustres is rather difficult work, because they dry so quickly. Have the silk dabber ready and close at hand, so as to lose no time. You might even apply a part of the lustre and pad quickly, and then proceed with the same, etc. Oil of lavender will be very helpful; a little of it mixed with the lustre (though not mixed in the bottle) will give it a little slower drying, and the padding will be more successful.

Insides of cups, bowls, etc., can be painted by pouring a small quantity of lustre into them, and rubbing it around with a silk dabber, to cover the desired surface. Be careful to have all the dabbers singed, as the lint would show badly on these colors. Place lustre pieces in the kiln in such a way that, kiln dust can not fall and adhere to them. In drying them before firing, remember that too great a heat would pulverize them.

In burnishing gold, do not rub over the lustres, as they would be easily affected and scratched. When thick, they will crackle off. Applied over fired colors they will lose their brilliancy unless the fired color is extremely light. Fired lustres can easily be removed with the liquid china eraser.

Give lustres a medium firing; and to produce a heavy effect, paint and refire them several times. When they are applied over gold, the gold must be burnished. Colors applied over them will give poor results, and the effect will be disagreeable. Over fired matt colors they will produce a rich, reddish, metallic effect, harmonizing well with gold and paste work. Lustres over gold, will also produce metallic effects, according to the color applied. For instance:

Dark green over gold gives a dark greenish bronze effect; light green over gold, a delicate Tiffany sheen effect; orange over gold, a purplish-bluish bronze tone; ruby, a strong, dark metallic effect. Lustres over liquid bright gold will be more brilliant, but the result will not be so satisfactory as over the Roman gold

Liquid silver lustre over light, fired colors, will have a frosted appearance that will look very well in connection with turquoise enamels, and paste and gold work. Liquid bright silver (not lustre), fired and covered with two coats of purple, gives a splendid deep maroon effect. Orange over ruby lustre will have a strong scarlet effect. This same orange will produce greenish tints over blue, dark green, olive, etc. Orange over iridescent rose will have a good bronze effect. Orange will crackle off, however ,if applied too thickly, and when under-fired will rub off. In this case, a coat of yellow and a good firing will cure the trouble. Orange over gold will have a purplish-bronze effect.

Yellow is generally a light tone and is mostly used for backgrounds or to mix with other colors, such as greens, blues, or grays, to produce a lighter tone. If a stronger yellow is desired, apply and refire it a number of times.

Light green is a greenish gray, which can be made more intense by applying it in several coats. This tint is used a good deal in connection with gold, being applied when gold is fired.

Rose over liquid bright gold will give a strong metallic effect. Rose and pink, if over-fired, will have a purplish tone. A light wash of yellow or light green over fired rose, gives a very pretty pearly effect. Rose makes a very good background for paste and gold work. Iridescent rose has touches of blue, pink, and gray. This is most attractive for an all-over tint for the insides of cups and bowls, etc. For this purpose do not pad, as the rougher the tint is applied, the more beautiful will be the effect.

Dark colors like purple, dark green, steel blue, and copper are apt to become spotted in the firing if not well protected from dust and humidity.

Mother of pearl and opal are not always reliable, and frequently fire off.

Yellow pearl is an iridescent color and very beautiful, having touches of light and deep tones.

Pigeon gray is a dark gray pearl, having iridescent touches of bluish and greenish color, such touches being produced by the roughness of strokes.

Green pearl is a greenish opal, very delicate if applied in one fire, and deeper if reapplied two or three times.

Two fired coats of black lustre covered by a third coat of ruby lustre, will make a very deep bluish-violet tone.

Ruby purple is a beautiful color, and when reapplied will make a very deep tone. It is mostly used in connection with paste and gold work. Ruby under dark or light green gives a splendid, iridescent, deep green, which makes an excellent ground for gold.

Steel blue is a very soft transparent color, as a rule, but sometimes fires as an iridescent, dark greenish-gray. It will combine well with black and silver for conventional designs. A coat of yellow over steel blue will have the effect of oxidized silver.

Copper is a color that is not used a great deal,

though it works well with a gold covering or over gold lustre.

White has no tint and will not show. It will be useful for washing over rubbing-off colors, or over light tints like rose, yellow, light green, etc., to produce a pearly effect.

Black lustre always requires two or three coats, and looks well with jewels and raised paste work.

Enamels applied over unfired lustres will take a pinkish tone, and some very good combinations may be effected.

Gold applied over unfired lustres will lose its brilliancy and will fire half matt.

Brown is a good color for banding.

Paste may be used over unfired lustres provided these are perfectly dry. Better results, however, will be obtained if they are fired before applying the paste.

Lustre applied over India ink will burn off. Gold pen-outlining over lustre produces a delicate and pretty effect. When blown on the china with a pulverizer they also make many novelties of decorations.

All the effects and combinations given above are fruit of our own experiences, which will, we hope, be a good guide to the students in this very difficult branch of decoration. But, above all, observe their changes and properties, keep account of the accidents, and you will begin to produce good things and find the work very interesting and attractive.

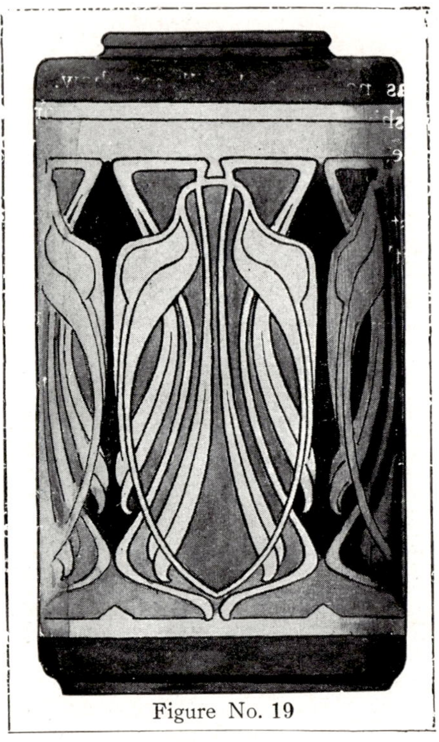

Figure No. 19

The above decorated piece, having been sent to
an important National Art & Craft Exhibit, received
the jury classification of "Very Good." We mention
this fact, only to explain to students the style of
decoration most appreciated by a very strict jury,
composed of the most selected designers in varied
branches of art and craft. While other subjects may
be more interesting and pretty to the public, **real art**

requires sober, well balanced lines, with easy intersection and befitting the shape of the china. The color effect of this vase was in royal blue, heavy at the top and bottom, and also between the main section of the subject. Within the ornament, where the shade appears of a middle-tone, the color is in gray green, while the ornaments themselves are in Copenhagen gray, very smooth. Outlines are in black, rather well defined. Should the student wish to make a good effect entirely different from the original one, the following colors will make a very harmonious and rich effect. Top and bottom, solid black; between designs, an even coating of auburn brown, rather dark, and the design, in a well padded shade of yellow brown. The color will be warm and good.

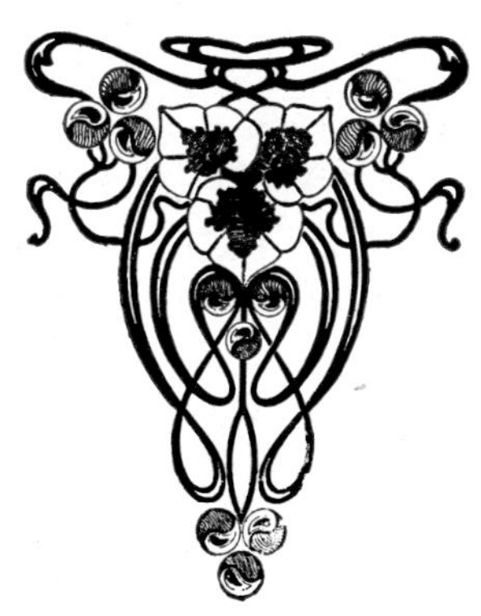

CHAPTER IV
GROUND-LAYING

This branch of work in china painting presents many difficulties, but its beautiful results will repay the student for all the time given to learning it.   By this process

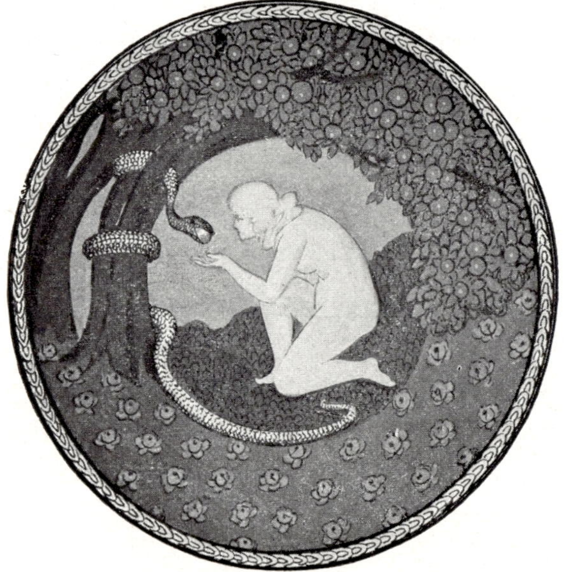

Figure No. 9

of applying the powdered colors to the china, over a coat of previously applied oil, a perfect flat and glazy ground is obtained.

The result will be not unlike a well padded, tinted ground, but still smoother and better.

The first requisite is a good quality of grounding oil, as upon this depends in great measure your success. It is best to buy a tinted oil, sold by the leading manufacturers. Shake the bottle well. Pour into a small dish enough oil to cover the desired space, having rather too much than too little. Stir the pure oil well with your knife, until all lumps or bubbles have disappeared; then take a broad, perfectly clean square brush, and apply the oil quickly over the space to be ground-laid with color. It does not require any particular skill for the strokes; only be careful to cover every little space. Have at least two good sized and rather soft pads, free from lint and ready for use. Now, with one of these pads, pad the oil all around and over and over again, until it will look like a smooth, soft tint. Repeat the work with the second pad; for, though this second padding may not be necessary, it will certainly improve the smoothness of the oil. Now, here is a special warning. If the oil appears uneven, spotted, or scratched, the color will show these same faults and marks. It would be safer to remove the oil and reapply it, than to try to remedy a fault on the padded oil.

Leave the oiled china undisturbed for half an hour or so, and then begin to apply the powdered colors. Have plenty of the latter on a large plate; hold the piece of china over it, horizontally, and with a piece of soft, clean cotton, take up as much color as possible and drop it over the part of the china covered with oil. Of course, if you hold your china vertically, the color will drop off, so keep it horizontal. Use plenty of color, and apply it by spreading over the oil, with a circular motion, over and over and very lightly.

Keep always a quantity of color on your cotton; this is to prevent the cotton itself from touching the oil and in this way rub the latter off. When the oil is evenly covered, repeat the dusting with fresh cotton, again and again, until no more color will adhere to it. Now, with a very soft, dry brush, remove all the superfluous color, and your ground is finished. If any design is to be cut out, do it now, or let it dry, according to the directions given in the chapter on cutting-out. This ground, if carefully done, will be heavy when fired, and will have a strong glaze. If you desire a medium heavy, or a light ground, add turpentine to the oil and mix them well; the more turpentine the lighter the oil, and naturally the less will be the color adhering to it. Light grounds may be repeated at the second firing, but it would be dangerous to attempt the repetition of heavy colors. It must be remembered that watery turpentine will interfere with the production of an even ground; since the water would dry in spots and absorb no color, making the tint imperfect. This mistake will only be discovered after the firing. In fact, many grounds will look very well and soft before firing, showing merely a solid, dusted surface; but the faults will all be very prominent after the china has been fired.

Powder colors taken from the vials are apt to be hardened from the packing, and may come up on your cotton or dusting brush in pieces, rather than in powder.

These pieces would scratch your oil and affect the ground. To prevent this, break up the powder well and if possible pass then through a sieve.

Different tints can be applied on a ground and blended together beautifully. Apply the lighter color first, and carry same slightly into the part which is to be occupied by the darker tint. In applying the darker color, soften it as it approaches the edge of the lighter tint, and be careful to avoid leaving a sharp line. Blend the lighter color over the darker one, and vice versa, so as to give a very smooth and soft appearance.

We must call attention once more to the fact that the greater the amount of turpentine mixed with the oil, the thinner will be the coat of powder adhering to it, and in consequence, the lighter the ground. For maroons, purples, pinks, and violets, use light grounds.

It is quite difficult to remedy any scratches on these grounds. If you attempt to fill in the scratches with moist colors, remember that grounds done by this method fire much darker than when colors are applied in the regular manner, and fill in your scratches with darker colors accordingly.

It is customary to dust the still unfired background with a light coat of flux or glaze to produce a more brilliant effect. This is not absolutely necessary in warm colors, such as reds, flesh tone, or browns; but it will improve blues and dark greens. Do not attempt to paint over the dry unfired ground; this would be very difficult indeed.

Ground-laying is done in the same way with matt

colors, with this difference: matt colors are naturally opaque, and therefore it will be easier to make them smooth and perfect. Use a trifle of turpentine with the oil for matt color dry grounds. The colors are so dull that it would scarcely show whether they are applied heavily or lightly and it is just as well, in that case, to have a medium weight ground.

Enamels cannot be safely ground-laid on account of the risk of chipping. Gold and silver can be ground-laid by applying first a coat of liquid bright gold or silver, as the case may be, and then applying the regular gold and silver in powder form, much in the same way as the color was applied to the oil. The first liquid coat should be diluted with a drop or so of oil of lavender to prevent its drying too quickly. This gold ground is the best surface for agate etching, having a rather subdued satin appearance, which will show off the brilliancy of the etching to good advantage.

There is another way of laying a good ground on china—with the assistance of a special apparatus, made on the principle of the air brush, so extensively used for crayon portraits. These grounds are beautiful, can be quickly made, and the different colors can be blended nicely. The only difficulty is that it requires a strong air pressure, to produce the necessary spray. This method is used extensively in large factories, where china and glass are decorated in large quantity.

CHAPTER V
MIXING OIL

HOW TO MAKE IT AND HOW TO USE IT

Mixing oil is used with powder colors. Have the desired quantity of powder color on the slab or palette, and pour a few drops of mixing oil over it; stir it well

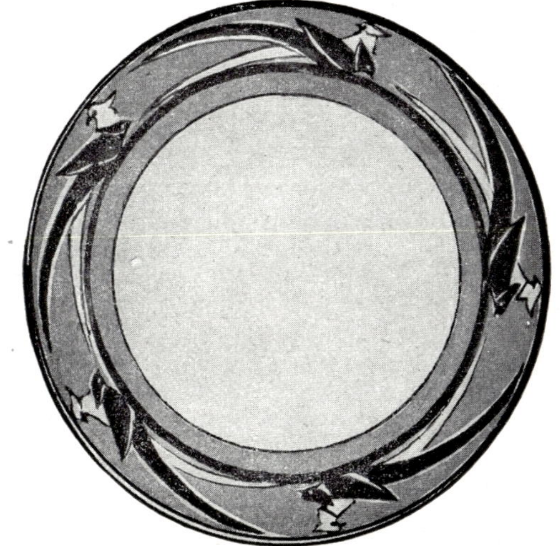

Figure No. 10

in a grounding way until the color has become perfectly assimilated and the mixture is smooth. The color should now have a semi-thick consistency. Too much oil on the colors will cause them to shrink and run, and to destroy the tints, giving a whitish, speckled appearance to the painting after the firing. Too much oil on a dark ground is apt to make the colors chip, gather dust and lint while you are at work, and run on the china. It is advisable to grind colors with a glass grinder to insure smooth and better results. Colors that have been ground several days before and left on the palette, may be used, provided they have been kept free from dust. For these add a very small quantity of diluting medium and remix them; by adding mixing oil to them every day, you will run the risk of having chipped or blistered colors. For this reason, tube colors had better be mixed with a diluting medium whenever any medium is necessary. Too much oil is also apt to oxidize purples, rubies, and dark browns. Be specially careful about the dark browns. The following three recipes for mixing oils are equally good, and are used by all the leading china artists.

Recipe I

1 part balsam of copaiba.
1 part oil of tar.
1 part lavender oil.

Recipe II

8 parts balsam of copaiba.
1 part oil of cloves.
1 part oil of lavender.

Recipe III

1 ounce fat oil of turpentine.
10 drops oil of cloves.

Fat oil of turpentine is made by evaporating the turpentine, pure. Put 1 pint of it in an open jar and leave it undisturbed until it becomes very thick, and the thicker the better. It will require more than one month to evaporate one pint of turpentine.

We desire to warn all students of the fact that drug stores do not always have fresh oils of this kind, their consumption being generally limited. Better results in painting are obtained with a fresh quality of materials, and manufacturers making a specialty of ceramic goods will, as a rule, sell enough to guarantee a reliable medium at just as cheap prices.

CHAPTER VI

GOLD AND HOW TO MAKE IT

There are many different recipes for making a good gold, but just as many disappointments; and the one paying for the sad experience, has learned nothing and generally has spoiled several pieces of china, without counting several greenbacks. Still, the difficulty of producing this metal increases the interest in the experimenting, and as we have worked for two years and ruined much gold before having any success in producing a good metal, we think we can advise more unfortunate brethren in the best and simplest methods yet known to dissolve and mix a reliable yellow gold.

Five pennyweights, or about one quarter of an ounce, of pure gold will be the proportions taken for this recipe. Ribbon gold may be bought from goldsmiths or assayers, and will dissolve more readily than gold coin. The following process will answer for both ribbon and coin gold, only for the latter allow double time for the dissolution in the acid. Put the gold into a large mouthed jar, without any rubber or iron at the edge of it. A one-quart fruit jar will answer. If the gold is in ribbon, cut it in small pieces. Cover the gold with two ounces of granulated salt of ammonia (ammonium chloride), dilute it with about half a pound of nitric acid, and cover the jar with a piece of glass. Do not close the jar with a screw cover, or any other tight way, but allow the cover to lie on the jar. Now take another jar (a pint fruit jar will do), and pour into it one-half pound of mercury, and over this three-quarters of a pound of nitric acid. Cover this jar with a piece of glass, just as you did the first jar. Place the two jars in a warm place, and leave them undisturbed over night.

We remember how curious we were on the morning of our first experiment, and how surprised to see some of the gold yet undissolved. We learned afterward that the cause of this was the cold night and the cold place in which the bottle was placed. When the atmosphere is warm the process of dissolving is quick; in fact, too warm a temperature will cause the liquid to boil over, and you will lose some of the gold.

The bottle containing the gold will show in the morning a yellowish liquid, which is called chloride of gold, and the metal should have disappeared completely.

If the temperature is low, the mercury may be found crystallized in the morning, in which case put it in a warm place and stir with a glass rod until clear and water-like.

This fact is apt to give the artist some trouble;

therefore, we would advise him to dissolve the mercury in the morning and when the gold is already dissolved.

The dissolution of the mercury takes only half an hour or so, and when completely dissolved, and not before, pour it into the gold bottle. Now, do not forget to protect your hands with rubber gloves.

Take the mercury bottle and pour its contents slowly into the gold bottle, and strong yellow fumes will issue from it. Cover the gold jar at once with the piece of glass, and leave it undisturbed. When the mixture has ceased boiling, which will be in about half an hour, the gold will be at the bottom or on top of the liquid and will look like a brown spongy mass.

Pour out the acid very slowly, holding the gold back with a glass rod. Now take your gold out and put it into a shallow dish or pitcher, having a prominent lip, so that the water which is used to wash the gold can be easily poured off without loss. Cover the gold with a pint of boiling water, which will destroy any salt that may have been left on the gold. Stir it constantly with the glass rod, and throw the water away carefully, being attentive not to lose any of the metal. Cover it with new boiling water again and again, so as to have washed the gold at least six times with it. Having thrown the last water away, put the gold on a glass slab and put it in a hot place to dry.

Weigh the dry powder, which should be exactly five pennyweights, as before. If you have lost some of it, reduce the proportions for flux, etc., that are given below. If the weight is correct, add ten grains of good gold flux, and five grains of silver in powder form. Moisten this combination with water, and grind the three together with a clean glass grinder, on a specially clean ground glass. This glass slab and also the grinder used for gold, should be used for this purpose alone.

Do not be afraid of grinding the gold too much. From half an hour to an hour is necessary, and the smoother the gold, the more will be the work accomplished with it. When very fine, dry it perfectly, and grind it again, with turpentine. Now re-dry it, and your gold is ready for use.

This quantity of powder can now be mixed with three and one-half pennyweights of good, fresh, thick oil, and this mixture, very well amalgamated, is the gold bought in paste form for the general use of china and glass painting. See Gold Work, which is amply treated in a separate chapter of this book.

Gold in powder or paste form, has either a very dark brown or a light auburn color, according to the time allowed for dissolving it. If the gold is placed near a hot stove, and therefore more quickly dissolved, its brown color will be very dark and nearly black. On the other hand, if it is placed in a moderate temperature, and is allowed about twelve hours for dissolving, its brown color will be light and warm.

No lampblack can be mixed with the gold without affecting its brilliancy, and the talk of putting lampblack on the gold is foolish and unfounded. It happens sometimes that small sheets of undissolved gold are found in the gold powder, which proves that the metal was not fully dissolved. Take the small pieces out and keep them for the next lot to be dissolved and put them in the acid with the metal.

If the acid comes in contact with your hands or clothes, wash with water immediately. Of all the different methods, this is the best and most practical way to prepare your gold, and though of course much experience is required, just as in any other line of work, still, rest assured, that a close adherence to these rules will be productive of good and quick results.

Imperfect oil in mixing or bad turpentine in grinding it will give imperfect gold.

Bad flux will reduce the wearing quality of the gold. The larger the proportion of the silver powder used in the gold the lighter will be the gold color. In fact, green gold is made by mixing one part of silver and three parts of unfluxed gold. Unfluxed gold is the same brown powder spoken of above, only ground without the 10 grains of flux; this is to be used on soft wares and over fired colors, whose glaze alone will be sufficient to hold the metal.

NOTE.—See other recipes for the making of gold on pages 37-133.

CHAPTER VII

RECIPE FOR BURNISH SILVER

Dissolve the desired quantity of silver ribbon or sheet silver (which may be bought of a silversmith) in nitric acid in the proportion of thirty ounces of acid to five dollars' worth of silver, adding a small quantity of warm water. Use a large mouthed jar, such as you would use for burnish gold.

When the metal is thoroughly dissolved, put a piece of copper wire into the mixture, which will precipitate the silver into a whitish powder. Pour off the acid and wash the silver very carefully in frequent changes of clear water. Cover the silver with strong ammonia and put it into a warm place until perfectly dry. Next add about one-tenth of its weight of bismuth subnitrate, grind well with water and dry. Finally, grind well with turpentine, and after allowing it to dry again, the silver is ready for use. It can be used with thick oil for paste form, and also in powder form for ground-laying purposes.

However, by mixing the rough, unground powder with balsam of capaiba and a trifle of oil of cloves, a very smooth silver paste will be attained, and in this case the decorator will do away with the tedious work of grounding. The silver so mixed requires a harder burnishing.

Note.—Pure nitric acid will not dissolve silver, but will do so with addition of water. It can also be precipitated by adding carbonate of soda until the acid is neutralized, and few drops of ammonia. If by adding a few more drops of ammonia the silver gives a purplish tone, wash again, as there is still some copper in the solution.

CHAPTER VIII

FIGURE PAINTING

This branch of painting, of itself rather difficult, has been made more so by a complicated method of working. Many unnecessary tints and the problem to apply them in the proper place, the difficulty of the blending, and

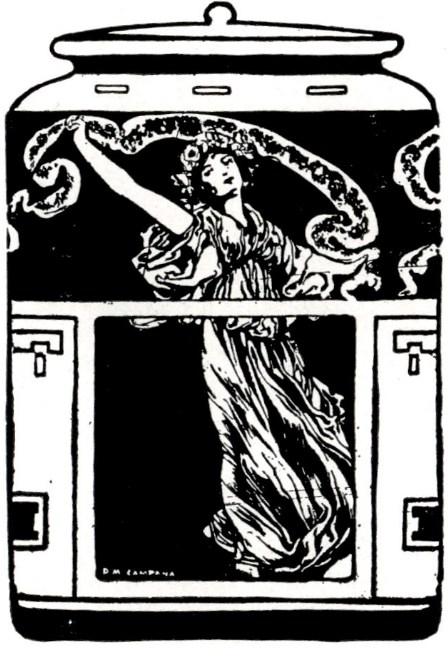

Figure No. 11

the strong probability of producing a miserable looking figure, etc., have discouraged many students from following a style of painting very interesting and valuable. It is our opinion that figure painting is the most admired and that this style would supplant all other decorations if proper application and a simplified method were taught to students of china painting.

Let us look back at the Egyption, Greek, Roman and Renaissance decorations of pottery, and we will find figures as the main subject, applied flat and in a decorative way.

These decorations are much admired, but apparently have not been followed. They are comparatively easy to produce and they open a large field with an unlimited number of subjects. In cut No. 9 a simple but effective specimen of this work may be seen. But as the flat figure painting is only supplementary and can be more easily produced, our aim here is to explain the easiest method to produce figures in their natural colors.

First of all, the student should endeavor to have a perfect drawing on the china, which drawing may be drawn on paper and traced on the vase, so as to have a clean, perfect line.

We will speak here of the flesh tone, and for this, the face will be taken as subject. From this, and using the same method, hands, feet, and full nudes can be painted. After the eyes, mouth, nose, etc., are drawn correctly, and as lightly as possible, take a lining brush and outline with flesh shadow, the eye lashes, the nostrils, the chin, ears, hair, etc., the outline to be extremely light. From this drawing, proceed to the shadows of the face, which are to be done in the same color, and must of course be done very smoothly. Now add a very little flesh gray on the edge of the flesh shadow color, toward the lighter part of the face. In other words, the gray is the neutral tone, between the light and the shadow; and this neutral tone may be observed on the face of persons having a good velvety complexion. Blend the colors well, but do not mix them, and keep the gray of a pure tone though very light. Too heavy a gray will turn out greenish in the firing, and spoil the figure. Outline lips with a soft touch of flesh tint. Paint the eyes and hair very lightly in the color desired, and fire.

In other words, paint the face in flesh shadow and flesh gray only, leaving the lights perfectly white, and fire. All this must be done smoothly and while the colors are fresh, in order to blend them well.

For the second firing, wash over the entire face with a light coat of flesh-soft-tint, pure, covering lights and shadows, and then proceed to reapply the latter with flesh shadow, while the flesh tint wash is still moist. Do not repeat the gray tone, which, if well done, will show through the covering of flesh tint as a soft, warm gray. Strengthen the eye lashes, paint the eyes of the desired color, the nose shadow, etc., retouch and cover the lips with a touch of flesh-soft-tint. Retouch the hair, and cut out the little high lights found on the subject, and fire. In other words, on first firing, use flesh shadow and flesh gray, and on second firing, flesh shadow and flesh-soft-tint.

On third firing touch up the shadows with flesh

shadow, strengthen the cheeks with a light coat of soft-flesh-tint, and use this same color to shade the lips. Finish the eyes, hair, etc., and fire.

As may be seen from this short explanation, no method of working could be simpler, and we have an ample number of examples to prove our assertion that, it is a method productive of good results. With only three flesh colors to work with the student is not so apt to become confused and the work is therefore easily accomplished.

A darker tone, for dark shadows on the eyes, etc., can be made by mixing flesh gray with soft-flesh-tint, and also by mixing this latter with flesh shadow.

Practice, of course, is necessary, but if this method of figure painting be compared with others, it will be found that it requires less time than any other to learn.

The color of the hair for a face of light complexion should be done with flesh shadow on first firing, painting only the shadows of the hair, and leaving the lights plain white. On second firing, wash over both lights and shadows with a light coat of yellow brown, and rettouch the shadows. For dark hair, use hair black, softened perhaps, with one-sixth part of banding blue.

For gray eyes use flesh gray, and for dark eyes use finishing brown.

For chestnut colored hair, use hair brown or finishing brown. All these colors can be mixed with other shades to suit the subject and the artist. There is one great fault that artists must guard against, and this is the putting of too strong a red on the face.

Strange to say, though we all notice a homely person, yet when we come to paint one, we become color blind and produce most abominable things, with red cheeks and crooked eyes, and perhaps several extra fingers or toes. Use your flesh sparingly, and do not in any case use yellows on your flesh tones. This is very disagreeable indeed. Also be very light on your gray tones.

In painting nude figures, work in the same manner as we explained for the painting of faces. Flesh shadow, flesh gray and soft-flesh-tint will answer the purpose, as stated before, for all figures.

For a brunette, accentuate the shadows and grays, but the soft-flesh-tint for the general flesh, will answer as well for light or dark complextions. We do not advocate the padding of flesh tints, but as the method of application is of little importance, for the reason that we admire the decoration and not the method used in doing it, we advise students to follow their own choice about padding, but to be exact in all that pertains to drawing and to be clean in what pertains to technique.

CHAPTER IX
OUTLINING

A very practical method of outlining on china and one which will save one or two firings, is the following: mix the outlining china color in powder form (either black, brown, green, or whatever color you wish) with water and add about two drops of mucilage or sugar syrup, mixing the two very well with a knife. With a clean lining brush, outline the design just as you would with water colors. The lines will dry quickly and will adhere fast to the china, so that nothing but water can remove them. These colors will be apt to dry on the palette, in which case add a drop of water and remix well. The outlines made with what might well be called water colors, since the colors are mixed with water, will remain perfectly intact. and will show through the regular oil-mixed colors, so that you can paint and repaint over them with these latter without fear of rubbing off the lines. The outlines will fire strong and clear, just as if they had been mixed with oil so that if the background is applied with regular oil-mixed colors, and the design cut out and tinted, a decorated piece of china can be obtained in one firing. Had you made your outlines in ink, the lines would have disappeared in the firing, while with this method, both ground and lines will show clearly. For this manner of outlining, use a brush, as water-mixed china colors do not flow very readily from a writing pen.

For pen outlining, with regular colors, mix these latters with regular mixing oil to the consistency generally used in painting. Add diluting medium to make the colors liquid enough to flow from the pen like ink. Experience of course is necessary; the oil may be too thick, and will not flow well, or it may be too liquid and drop from the pen. If you will find the right consistency, this mixture will work perfectly. It will keep moist as long as desired, and will not clog the pen. Any clean steel writing pen will answer the purpose. Use a small pen for small lines, and a large pen for larger drawings. A small brush can also be used for this work.

Ink outlining is done with ink for china, which will fire away without affecting either the colors or gold, though traces of the ink will show when lustres are applied over them. Apply it from the bottle, like ordinary ink, and when this is dry, apply the china colors, which will not affect the lines.

One way of making a broad outline, is to paint the line itself with grounding oil, mixed very thoroughly with a small quantity of lamp black. Draw your lines well and dust the powdered color over them. Fire before applying any other tint over these lines. This method is practical for banding as it insures a very even color effect.

Good gold outlining can be done by mixing pure Roman gold with the diluting medium. Use no turpentine or liquid bright gold. Pure Roman gold mixed with diluter can be used either with a pen or brush; it will not dry, or clog the pen, and will work freely. Burnish silver can be used in the same manner.

Lustre and liquid bright gold outlining can be done with either pen or brush.

All color outlining can be done over fired colors, golds, lustres, and silvers.

Too thick a line will chip off.

Outlining in color can also be done over unfired dry tints, also over unfired but well-dried Roman gold. For outlining over unfired lustres, mix your powder color with water as stated above. Turpentine or oil will easily spread and spoil them. Gold outlining can also be made with powder gold mixed with lavender oil, but still better with diluting medium.

CHAPTER X
GOLDS

Dissolved gold, for china painting, is a brown powder; and the brown gold paste ordinarily used by china artists is this same powder mixed with oil. All the necessary information and formulas for dissolving and mixing gold will be found under a separate heading in this book. (See Chap. VI.)

Gold bought in paste form is usually hard and dry. A special brush should be kept for gold work only. Dip the brush into clean turpentine or oil of lavender, the latter preferred, and rub the gold paste with it briskly, until you have a thick brown color. This is applied to the china.

If the gold paste is very dry, pour a few drops of turpentine or oil over it, and mix it well with a palette knife to a sort of half-thick consistency. A drop of bright gold will soften the Roman gold quickly, but in that case use no turpentine.

For softening gold quickly, hold it over the fire, adding the desired turpentine afterward; it is our experience, however, that gold softened in this way becomes much harder after it has cooled and works unsatisfactorily.

ADDITIONAL NOTE.—Red gold is made by adding 5% of red oxide of iron and 3½% of purple of cassius to the pure gold powder.

GREEN GOLD by adding 10% of silver and 5% oxide of chrome.

Roman gold is used on hard white china; unfluxed or hard gold is used for soft ware such as Belleek or English china, and also over fired colors. Unfluxed gold over hard white china would rub off.

A very practical method of working in gold is to apply liquid bright gold at the first firing, and Roman gold at the next. The former will make a good foundation for the latter, and it has been proven that the glaze substance in the bright gold will make the combination good and wearing.

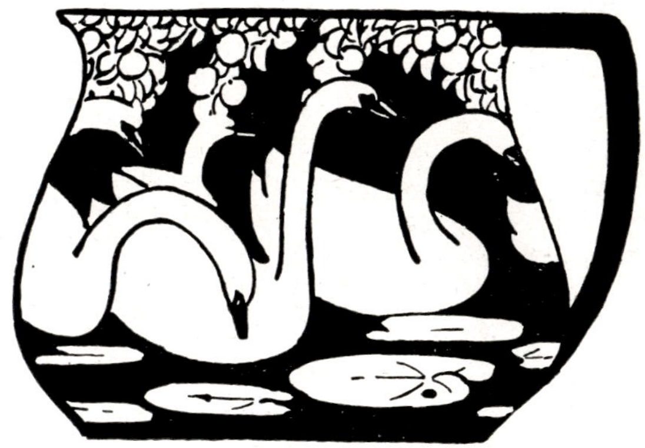

Figure No. 12

Gold will rub off in burnishing if underfired, and will weaken and fade away if overfired. It will stand a medium firing. If possible, apply the gold in the last two firings. As fire is apt to injure gold, it will be necessary to reapply it at each additional firing, should you be obliged to fire your china again. If you neglect to do this you may find yourself obliged to refire the china, merely on account of the gold.

Be careful to avoid handling the fired unburnished gold, as dust and perspiration from your fingers will show badly. This is one reason for advising you to burnish the gold after each firing before working or handling the china. Burnish the gold before applying lustres over it.

If the gold looks dull or dirty, impure turpentine or an unclean brush is the cause of it; or perhaps the china was dusty, or the gold was mixed and remixed too often. Mix only as much gold as you will use at that particular time, leaving the rest of it untouched on the slab.

In burnishing your gold with a glass burnisher, remember that the little glass fibers, if left on the china and refired, will eat away the decorations and leave bad marks. Therefore wash your article well after burnishing, and burnish it away from your place of work, so that the glass fibers may not get on the palette, as they could be lost in the colors and have just as bad an effect when those colors are fired.

Gold may be applied over unfired paste, provided the latter is perfectly dry; but, in order to be surer of good results, fire the paste first, and apply the gold afterward. If gold is applied too thick, it may peel off or blister.

Gold is often applied to plates or cup edges with the tip of the finger, by rubbing the gold evenly all around. Fired gold can be removed with the liquid china eraser.

Never use turpentine with liquid bright gold, nor with Roman gold if liquid bright gold is mixed with it.

Gold dusting is done by applying the powdered Roman or unfluxed gold over a coat of liquid bright gold. This latter dries quickly and should therefore be applied quickly, so that there will still be enough moisture for the powder to adhere to. The effect of this will be a dull finish, which makes such a splendid ground for agate etchings.

Roman gold mixed with liquid bright silver will give the effect of platinum. Use gold pure (unfluxed) on Belleek ware, and do not mix it with liquid bright gold.

Green gold is made by mixing burnish silver with unfluxed gold, in the proportion of one of silver, to two of gold.

Gold can be applied over fired silver, or silver over fired gold. One metal makes a good foundation for the second one.

It often happens that gold applied on Belleek ware. fires with a small wavy, grainy surface. This is caused by the moving of the glaze on the pottery itself during the process of firing. and such an effect cannot be remedied. To avoid this fire very lightly.

An economical decorator should clean gold slab and gold brushes with small pieces of rags, collect them in a small receptacle. and when a sufficient amount or rags is made, they should be burned and their ashes carefully gathered up. These ashes brought to a gold essayer, will be placed in a crucible and at high heat cleaned of

ADDITIONAL NOTE.—There is made a gold powder, of the same color as the real gold metal, and this is very appropriate for gold dusting.

all foreign substances. The gold always remains, and can be sold as gold or dissolved for further use, as stated in the chapter on how to make gold.

CHAPTER XI
MATT COLORS

These colors are opaque, and have a velvety surface, when fired, much like the unscoured gold. They can be prepared and applied just as other china colors are; but they are seldom used for anything but backgrounds, and in this case they are usually applied by the dusting process. They will stand any amount of firing without fading. They can be used in connection with ordinary colors, or can even be mixed with them; though in the latter case they lose part of their natural dullness. By applying lustres over matt colors, a reddish opaque effect will be attained, which harmonizes well with paste and gold work.

A beautiful bronze effect is produced by outlining or stippling gold over fired matt colors. It is also possible to paint with matt colors by mixing them with white, using them much as oil or guache painting colors are used.

It sometimes happens that a matt color will rub off after firing, especially if it is used thickly as a background. A very light coat of the matt color, mixed with a small amount of some regular vitrifiable china tint, will suffice to fasten the ground. This wash may be stippled on, or blown on with a pulverizer, or if the faulty colors are not too soft, apply with a large square shader as evenly as possible.

Paste and gold can be applied over fired matt colors, using unfluxed gold over the paste or Roman gold, if this is applied directly on the color itself.

It must be remembered that since these colors are opaque they will not permit any design to show through when fired. Any design that is supposed to be applied to these colors must be cut out. (See Cutting out.) Silver works successfully over matt colors; and vitrifiable china colors can be applied over fired matt tints.

It is not advisable to use matt colors on table ware or on any other article that should frequently be washed. These paints retain grease, dust, etc., and would soon lose that delicate velvety effect which is the peculiar charm of their nature.

Matt colors can be made by mixing the general china colors with a certain quantity of oxide of zinc. Some colors will need one-fifth of the oxide, some one-sixth and some one-fourth. Different makes and different tints require different proportions, and it would be unsafe to give one rule for all makes. Grind them well together with turpentine and dry them before you use them on the china. The decorator should make few experiments so as to find the proper quantity of zinc required.

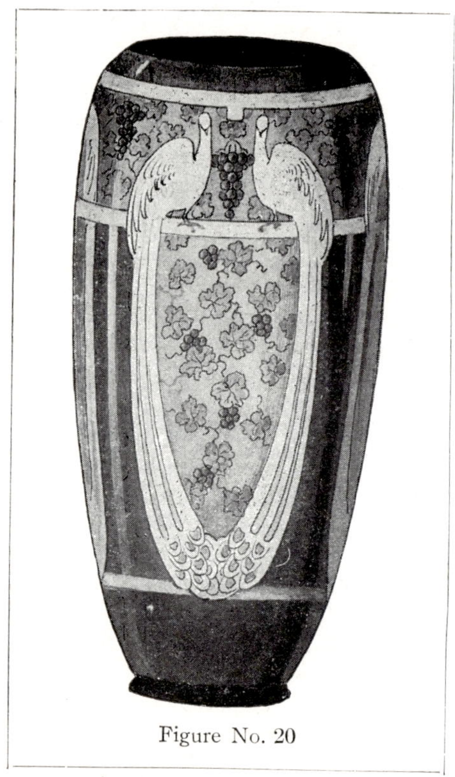

Figure No. 20

THE WHITE PEACOCK VASE.
By D. M. Campana.

The above design is very popular with the public, and is painted in a warm general effect. The general ground of the lower and side parts of the vase is in deep red brown, very smooth and dark. The little grapes are in banding blue, medium heavy outlined in royal blue. The small leaves are in flesh shadow, also stems. The background around the foliage at the broad border on top and between the peacock tails is in imperial ivory, dusted (when dry) with rose salmon. Foliage is outlined in ruby purple. The eyes on the peacock feathers are in Copenhagen blue; and these two colors are also used for the outlines of the feathers. The band at the top edge, also the one in which the peacocks stand are in a very delicate wash of air brown (smooth). The peacocks, but for the outlines, are perfectly white. Before each firing, when the colors are very dry, dust the whole with pearl gray and fire with a good glaze.

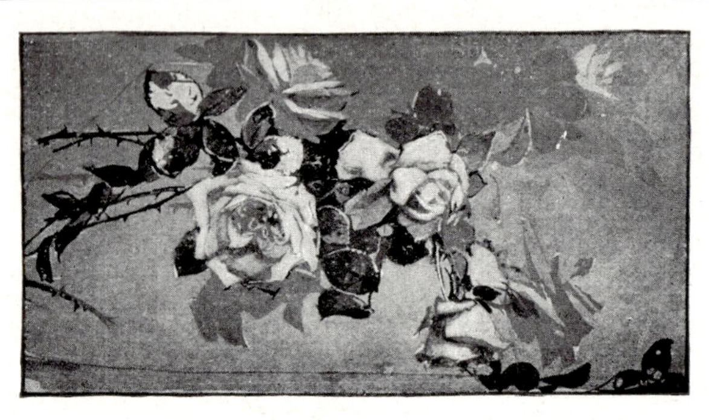

Figure No. 13

CHAPTER XII
FLOWER PAINTING

There is so vast a number of flowers, and **their** colors are so varied, that it would require more space to describe them than could possibly be afforded within the limits of this little book, which must of necessity treat all topics very generally. We can undertake only to outline the results of our own experience in painting the most popular flowers, such as roses, chrysanthemums, violets, daffodils, poppies, etc. A dark rose or an American beauty may be painted successfully as follows: paint the dark center of the rose and the broad masses of shadow in crimson purple, mixed with about one-sixth part of darkest green. Paint the half-shadows with pure crimson purple, and leave the lighter parts plain white.

The colors should be smooth, though of medium

thickness. For the second firing, wash over all the shadows with pure crimson purple and wash over the light parts with American beauty colors. Detail the petals with crimson, being careful to keep the shape of the rose as accurately as possible, then fire.

On third firing, if such is necessary, retouch with the same colors and be careful to keep the colors pure.

We find that dark roses frequently oxidize if black or brown is mixed with the purples; but it is our own experience that dark green or peacock green will be much safer tints to use with ruby or purples in order to produce the desired dark effect. These same colors are also successfully used to paint dark cherries, draperies, etc.

Pink roses are painted in rose colors, and it will be better to use these colors pure and not too thick.

A very soft, delicate effect is produced by dusting a little brown-green toward the shadow part of the rose before the second firing and let some of it run over into the background. Keep the centers a pure rose color. Roses, pinks, and peach blossoms will chip off if the color is put on too thick.

The shadows of white roses are to be painted in either light brown-green, or ashes of roses, or with a light neutral tint, made by mixing two parts of black to one part of blue. The center may have a pink or yellow-brown tone. The center can be dusted when the color is quite dry. Keep the shadows even and light, and paint the rose in one color, if possible; as this may be modified by dusting.

For yellow roses, use brown green for the shadows and yellow brown for the center and reflections.

For field poppies, use poppy red or yellow red in the lighter places, and dark pompadour or violet of iron for the shadows. Do not apply the colors too thick on the first firing; it is better to go over the colors again. Reds, when too thick, lose their brilliancy.

Poppy centers are dark green with little black dots.

Violets are painted with violet colors, and the tints can be reduced by adding banding blue to make the color more bluish, or ruby, which will give a warmer purplish cast to the violet color. In fact, equal parts of ruby and banding blue make a very good violet color. A good violet color may also be obtained by mixing two parts of violet of gold and one part of banding blue. The center of the violet is yellow brown. The petal of the single violet will look best if made in one stroke. The same colors are used for double violets. Black mixed with violet will give a dark tone, but will not be clear; it is better to apply the violet color repeatedly until the color is of the required depth.

Paint the shadows of daffodils for the first firing with light brown-green and the shadows in the center with light yellow-brown, leaving all lights plain white. On second firing wash the petals with light lemon yellow and the center with egg yellow.

For forget-me-nots, use deep blue green or turquoise blue.

For nasturtiums, use yellow red, blood red, yellow

brown or albert yellow, according to their various colors.

We have attempted to give here a color scheme for flowers of different colors, and we should advise following the same method for all other flowers which space prevents even mentioning. For instance, for white lillies or white daisies see white roses; for peonies, see either dark or light roses, according to the color; and for yellow daisies, see daffodils. In any case, paint shadows alone for first firing, keeping light parts perfectly white. On second firing, wash your main tint all over, detail your shadows, and cut out the small, sharp high lights.

CHAPTER XIII
LEAF PAINTING

It frequently happens that an artist's chief attention is so centered upon painting his flowers and fruits that but little thought is given to the leaves. They are usually considered the easiest thing to paint and of but little importance to the decoration in general. The weakness of a painting is therefore frequently detected by the handling of the leaves, which really require quite as much study as flowers or fruit, and enhance or spoil a work of art, according to the attention and skill bestowed upon them. It would be impossible to give here an exact rule for the disposition of the leaves, as this depends much on the movement of the decoration and the shape of the china. Leaves must be crisp and simple, and the fewer strokes used in painting them the better the result. Small leaves should be done in one flat stroke, figure 14.

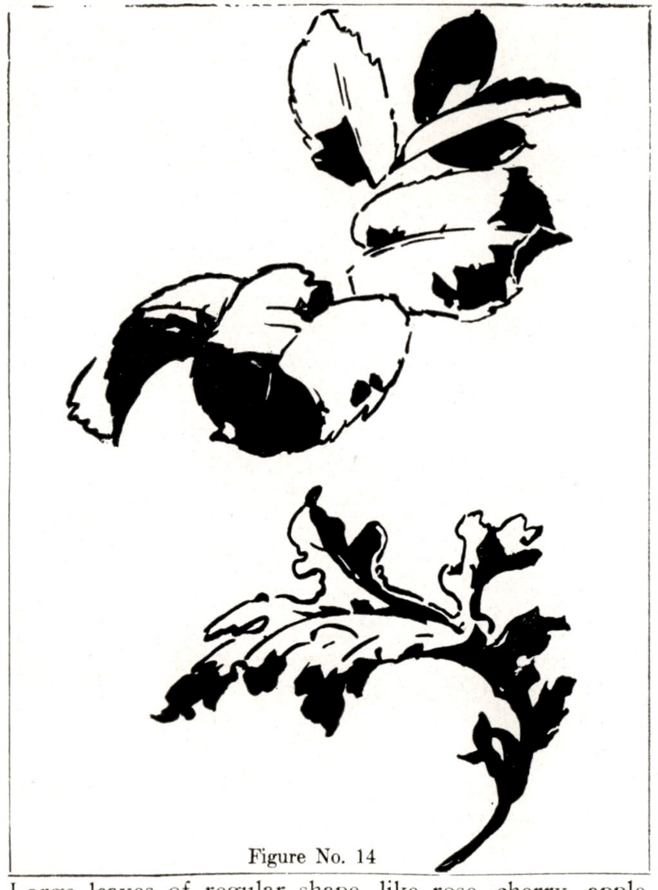

Figure No. 14

Large leaves of regular shape, like rose, cherry, apple, iris, tulip, etc., can be easily made in two strokes, one of a light and one of a darker color, leaving all detail to be applied on second firing.

Broken leaves, like poppy, crysanthemum, currants, grape leaves, etc., need more strokes, of course, but the student should attempt to simplify even these as much as possible. It is a common error to apply the lightest parts of leaves and flowers first, and the shadows in the successive firings. This is contrary to the very fundamental rules of art. It is shadows that bring out the roundness of a subject. The lights are only supplementary contrasts.

What an effect would a face make if the only color applied on it, were the pinkish tone of the cheeks, and there were no eyes nor nose, which form the character of the face? In looking at a distant landscape, the eye will perceive the darker parts at first, and many of the lighter tones will unconsciously escape the attention.

Painting the dark parts alone, will give an effect sufficient to explain the character of the painting, though it is well to remember that a subject is always composed of both light and shade. But why not begin with that which gives character to a subject—the shadows? This is, as stated before, a primary and fundamental rule in every branch of painting. Paint the shadow of the leaf first, always, of course, keeping in mind the special character of the subject. Give to this darker part the right form and strength, and leave the rest of it plain white. In the second firing, cover the whole leaf with the light green desired, and detail with the darker color. The lighter tints can be applied in the succeeding firings, and by blending over the shadows, this tint will produce a soft effect.

This rule applies equally well to the painting of flowers, fruit, and figures. It would be difficult to assign different colors for the various kinds of leaves, as they are constantly changing color. Yellow green, apple green, peacock green, moss green, deep blue green,—all make good tints for the lighter parts, while shading green, brown green, darkest green, etc., make good colors for shadows. For autumn leaves use yellow brown, Meissen brown, and pompadour red.

CHAPTER XIV
ENAMEL WORK

Relief enamels are used in a number of ways, and will improve or spoil the decoration according to their proper or improper application. Aufsetzweiss, either in a tube or in powder form, will make a reliable white enamel.

Tube enamel, which is already moist, should be diluted with clear turpentine to a semi-liquid point and then reduced to the working consistency by breathing upon it.

Powder enamel must be well ground with turpentine, and, while still liquid, remixed with a small amount of fat oil. Breathe upon it, stirring with a knife, until it is of the desired thickness. This desired thickness is an important point in enamel work. The enamel must be of such a consistency that it can be applied in a long, full stroke, while at the same time it must have enough strength to preserve a high, round appearance on the china, which high appearance is the beauty of this branch of china decoration, just as it is of paste work. If the enamel is too thick, however, the handling will be difficult, while if too thin, it will flatten and possibly chip. Some experimenting, therefore, is necessary. Enamel is of the right consistency when a string of it will hang from the knife while mixing it, or when it will keep its erect form if piled up in a little heap.

Use a long red sable brush, and by putting it under the enamel, scoop it up, so that a certain quantity will hang on to the brush. Now apply it in scroll or dot fashion, being careful that only the enamel and not the brush touches the china; and try to produce a round cord-like line or high round dots. The dots will look pointed, but will round off in the firing. Do not attempt to repeat strokes while working; better do the work over.

Enamels will harden while working, and then a drop of turpentine must be added. Breathe upon it again, and proceed with the work. Too much oil will chip the enamel; if this is too oily, dry it on a piece of silk. If the enamel should chip in the firing, scrape it off and reapply.

Enamels should be fired once, or perhaps twice. Too many firings will cause them to chip off, though this is also caused by insufficient mixing. These colors will not chip off on Belleek or any other soft glazes. It is unsafe to use enamels that are not freshly mixed.

If applied to table ware or to any frequently used

piece, they will wear off. Let the enamel dry naturally and thoroughly before firing, to prevent chipping.

Tinted enamels can be bought, or mixed by adding one-fifth of the desired color to four-fifths of the white enamel. Blue, green, pink, and ruby mix well; reds and browns will either disappear or make a very disagreeable tint. Mix them well; they will fire darker. White enamels can be tinted by applying a light wash of color over them. They can be applied over unfired colors, or over fired gold. They will also fire well over fired lustres; but if the lustres are unfired, the enamel will have a slightly reddish tone.

A horn knife is desirable for mixing enamels, but this is not absolutely necessary. Flat enamels are called the broad flat grounds, and are applied as follows: Mix the white enamels, according to the directions at the head of this chapter. Add to this one-fifth of the desired color and one-eighth of flux. Dilute this mixture with oil of lavender, until the whole is of a fluid consistency, and mix it thoroughly. Apply this with a large square brush. Do not meddle with it, but let it flatten naturally. The strokes of the brush, will rather improve the **effect**. This ground will appear a little higher after firing, **and** only one firing is advisable.

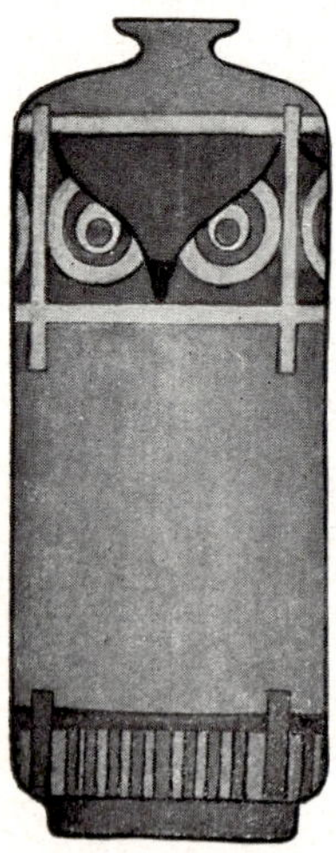

Figure No. 15

In applying several flat enamels on one piece of china, be careful not to let one run over the other. Dry each one, and separate them by a heavy line.

The following colors make very pretty enamel tints when mixed in the proportion of one-quarter or one-fifth of color to about four-fifths of enamel, adding perhaps one-tenth of flux.

For pink enamel, use peach blossom or ruby; for blue enamel, use turquoise blue or deep blue green; for yellow, use Albert yellow; for green, use peacock green or Russian green.

There are also several special enamels which cannot be composed, but can be bought from manufacturers. Coral red enamel, Mazarine blue enamel, black enamel, etc., are beautiful and reliable. Do not fire enamels too heavily. Enamels are also good for filling broad cracks and nicks in the china. In this case add to them one-sixth of china cement for mending.

Enamels for glass decorations should be properly made in mixing the white enamel with the *matt colors*. These matt colors will minimize the trouble of bubbling, which fault is so often the cause of the bad enamels seen on glass work. Glass enamels will also work better when mixed with water instead of oil. The oily substance makes them chip off, while the water will remedy this trouble almost entirely.

CHAPTER XV
FRUIT PAINTING

A very important point in the painting of fruit, as well as of flowers, is the application of the proper leaf, in accordance with their many different species. We very often observe decorators painting blackberries, grapes, plums, currants or other fruit and adorn all of them with the invariably ragged leaves always alike in shape, which have no earthly reason to be unloaded upon any innocent fruit or flower. It would make a similar impression if a tin can should cover the dignified head of Venus of Milo.

In painting, we warn the student to observe the law of nature above all—even to the very smallest details. Fruits, like flowers, are varied enough to fill a volume with their description, and we must confine our directions to painting the fruits most commonly used in china decoration, and the student can use these as types for colors. Blackberries, like wild cherries, are to be painted in black, for the first firing, painting only the dark side of the berries and leaving the high lights plain white. On the second firing, wash all over the berries with a light coat of black and banding blue in equal proportions, adding perhaps a little purple to give warmth. Cut out one or two high lights in the center of the berries, and refire.

If a third firing is necessary, follow the same method, but do not apply the black too heavily, as dark colors is very apt to chip off if it is of more than ordinary thickness.

A beautiful dark cherry color can be obtained by painting the cherry in dark green for the first firing, and washing it over with a coat of crimson purple at the next firing. Do not forget to cut out the high lights, which are especially strong in all smooth-skinned fruit.

Red cherries can be painted by using yellow or poppy red, for the lighter parts, and dark pompadour for the shadows. A good color for deep cherries is violet of iron.

Dark pompadour is the color to be used for currants; it should be kept thin, and clear high lights must be left. Many artists use yellow-red for this fruit.

Plums are painted with banding blue and crimson purple, using about three parts of the former, and one of the latter. Repeat this tint on second firing, and then give a light wash of black to the shadow parts.

For dark blue grapes use about one-half of banding blue, and one quarter each of purple and black, preserving a strong contrast between light and shade.

Violet of iron is a good shadow color for red grapes, and dark pompadour, mixed with about one eighth of ruby, is to be used for the lighter parts; being exceedingly careful to keep this tint really light.

The shadows of green and white grapes are to be painted with a light wash of olive green, while a light touch of egg yellow will be good for the transparent parts underneath the grapes. Leave enough high light, and cover the whole fruit with a delicate wash of ivory yellow on second firing.

Crab apples are to be painted brown-green in the shadow parts, and light touches of yellow-brown and yellow-green will be good for the lights. On second firing, add the reddish tones in yellow-red and dark pompadour.

Strawberries are to be painted in dark pompadour, for the shadows, while a very light coat of light pompadour will suffice for the lighter parts. Right here it is best to warn the artist again, to work up the shadows of whatever subject she is painting, for the first firing leaving the lighter parts to be washed over on successive firings.

Oranges are yellow-brown, usually dark on one side, light on the other.

Lemons are shaded in brown-green, and have a thin coat of lemon-yellow on the lights.

Red raspberries are to be painted in dark pompadour, as this color approaches their delicate tint more closely than any other.

Moss green is a good shadow color for green gooseberries, and apple green will do very nicely for the lighter parts of this fruit. Gooseberries, when ripe, have a pinkish cast, which is quite difficult to obtain. A light dusting of peach blossom over very lightly painted dark pompadour will make a pretty pink tone, well adapted to this fruit.

Peaches are to have their shadows painted in brown-green, which must be blended into the lights with a light wash of bluish violet color. Wash over the pinkish parts with a thin coat of dark pompadour, and then fire. On second firing wash over the whole of the fruit, with a mixture consisting of two parts of ivory yellow, to one part of yellow-brown; then strengthen the shadows and the red parts.

We must remind the student not to attempt quick results by using thick colors; apply colors sparingly; rely upon frequent firings to obtain strength of tints. Fruit or flowers painted with repeated applications of color will appear soft, and the glaze and transparency will be much superior.

The dusting, of which we have spoken under a separate heading, will be of great value in obtaining the delicate flushings and blendings so necessary in all naturalistic decoration, and when your fruit and ground are painted, apply light dustings of powder colors (apply with cotton or dry square shader), light pinks, delicate yellow-brown, greens, etc., rubbing lightly over fruit and background, producing a soft relation of tints, and a more harmonious effect.

CHAPTER XVI
CHINA REPAIRING

Many an imperfect piece of china has been completely ruined through unskillful repairing; when, if its cracks and nicks had been properly covered, the china would have been quite as useful as a perfect piece.

To repair a piece of china that has been cracked through and through, use "cement to be fired," mixed with water, until nearly liquid. Apply it to the crack repeatedly, so as to let the china absorb as much of it as possible; then wipe away all the surplus, and fire. This cement contains quite a good deal of flux, and will affect any color covered with it. It will always prove satisfactory when applied nowhere except just inside of the cracks.

If the article to be repaired is broken into many pieces, tie them together with asbestos cord before applying the cement to be fired, and fire with the asbestos. Asbestos will not leave a mark on hard china, and only a slight one on Belleek ware; but even this can be prevented by firing very lightly, and the cement will be quite as effective.

It must be remembered that this cement has no body and will do nothing toward filling in a space; it melts completely and holds the pieces together. If the crack is wide, apply the cement first, as explained before; let it dry, and then fill in the crack with enamel mixed with either oil or water.

To imitate the color of the decoration through which the crack comes, add a bit of the desired color to the enamel, being careful to remember that tinted enamels are rather darker after firing than before.

Fill in a nick with enamel mixed with one tenth of flux. After this is fired, it may be covered with paste and gold, and the fault will be completely obliterated.

By mixing one part of flux to nine parts of very finely grated china, a good filling will be produced for large cracks, or for places from which small pieces of china are missing. It must be very carefully applied, and dried before firing.

Paste and gold work will cover up cracks very nicely.

Unless the china is actually apart, the cement need be applied to only one side.

For a cracked vase, apply the cement by letting it

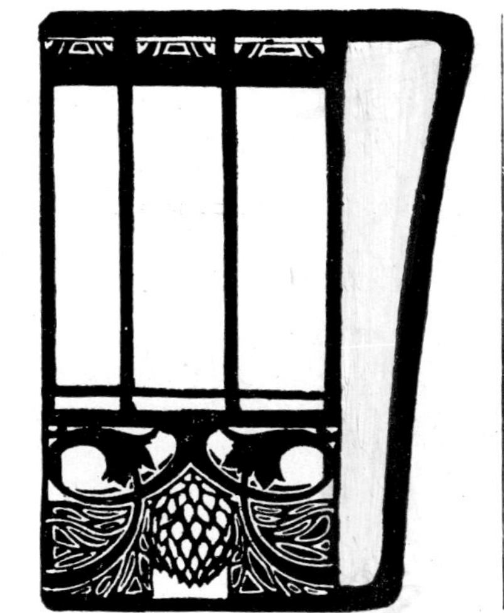

Figure No. 16

run along the inside of it only, but on a platter, apply it on the outside, or, if desired, on both sides.

Black spots and pin holes can be filled in with enamel.

China can also be repaired by using a cold cement, which should not be fired. Apply the cement with a stick, on the edges of both pieces, and put them together very carefully. Set the china aside, so that it will remain undisturbed until dry. If there are many pieces, join two or three, and let them dry, and gradually add on the others until the article is complete. Allow two days for an ordinary good drying, without artificial means, before handling.

A strong cold cement is made by mixing two parts of cheese to one part of powdered lime, adding water until the mixture is of a semi-liquid consistency. Mix and grind it with a knife until it has become tacky. Apply this to the edge of the china, and join the pieces carefully, allowing one day for it to dry.

Many large crockery houses use this cement exclusively, and find it very satisfactory.

CHAPTER XVII
TINTING

A broad tinting brush or square shader should be used for tinting, and one color or a combination of colors may compose a tint.

To obtain the best results, use freshly mixed colors; these work smoother and easier. Apply the tint as smoothly as possible, but should this not be sufficiently even, pad it with a cloth or silk pad, according to the thickness of the tint. Some colors will be found more gritty than others and therefore more difficult to pad. Yellow-brown, brown-green, apple-green, dark pompadour, and pink, are rather stony colors, and in order to pad them more successfully it will be found necessary to dampen the pad slightly with mixing oil.

When working with a smoother tint, it will be sufficient to tint the pad with the color by gently touching with the pad the color on the palette. When the tint is dry or nearly so, a dusting of colors will improve and deepen the effect. (See the article on Dusting.)

Tinting, when applied to a background for natural subjects, is also called flushing.

Light, delicate tints of pinks, grays, and greens, well combined and slightly blended over the edges of flowers or fruit to soften the latter, will be very effective. In applying backgrounds to natural subjects, always make it a rule to use similar colors for the background as are used in the subject itself, possibly by adding other little tints which will, if properly applied, enhance the beauty of the general effect.

CHAPTER XVIII
DUSTING

We explained in the article on "Underglaze Effects" the method of dusting the colors in order to produce a strong glaze. We also explained in the chapter on "Groundlaying" the method of applying powdered color for heavy and light grounds. The dusting we now refer to, is a process similar to the one used for underglaze effects, but with the use of varied tints, and for the purpose of altering or strengthening the tints already applied with wet colors. Suppose, for example, that the decoration is in light ivory or green and that a warmer tint is desired; dust the yellow-brown or yellow-red, or any other warm color on the already dry decorations.

Apply it with a pinch of cotton or a large dry brush, rubbing the powder gently; the small quantity adhering to the china will produce the desired effect.

Many colors can be applied by this method and blended into one another, producing either a good flushing of soft delicate tones, or a strengthening of heavy grounds, with dark greens, purples, blues, and browns.

Dusting of this sort is frequently used to soften and darken roses and other flowers. In that case, it is not necessary to limit the dusting to the subject, but allow the powder to blend the flower with the background, producing a very soft and pleasing effect. A light dusting of flesh tone on the cheek of a figure will have a very good result. In fact, much harshness and uneven padding can be covered by dusting, and any artist will be well repaid for the time spent in experimenting with the dusting of colors.

It must be particularly remembered that the decorations should be dusted before any gold or silver is applied, so that the metal (which is generally tacky) may not retain any of the little particles, as these would mar the brilliancy of the gold or silver. But for little necessary details it is possible to paint a complete subject well by the dusting process only. Of course, this would require several firings and careful handling, the dry colors being always applied with a dry brush of a size in proportion to the space to be covered.

CHAPTER XIX
CHIPPING OF COLORS

The chipping of colors is, in most instances, due to carelessness in the application of the colors to the china. We have, however, seen many cases in which the chipping was caused by an imperfection in the china itself; the latter may have such an unusually thin glaze, that the colors can not normally adhere to it in the firing.

The colors most likely to scale off are browns, dark greens, ruby, purple, pinks, and blacks. Yellow, light greens, blues, reds, and grays very seldom give trouble of this kind. Nor is chipping likely to occur with soft china, like Belleek or English ware, but very often with French or any other hard china.

A reliable safeguard against the chipping of colors is evenness in its application. Outlining in dark colors very often scales off on account of its uneven thickness. Avoid lumpy strokes, and remember that extraordinary thick colors will not produce heavier tints. The colors will only lose their brilliancy and will chip off quickly.

In mixing colors, be careful not to have them look gritty. Mix and grind them well, and you will have overcome one of the principal causes of chipping.

Too oily a color is dangerous; and this also applies to colors left to harden on the palette and remixed day after day. Too much oil is injurious.

There is no good way to remedy a chipped piece, and of all the faults or imperfections that occur in china painting this may be called the worst. By retouching and filling in the bad places, and then refiring, a fair result will be attained, but the glaze will always appear different. Furthermore, in the refiring, other parts may be affected and cause more trouble. If it is possible to cover the chipped places with enamel or paste and gold, use these means.

To avoid an extra firing, and to remedy faults by a method somewhat dishonest, mix powdered color with copal varnish and apply it thickly over the bad places. Apply it smoothly and carefully, and when this is dry, the color will make a fair imitation and will keep its brilliancy for a long time. Of course, this should not be fired. Blistering of colors is caused by bad oil, and will have the same bad effect on heavy or medium heavy tints. In this case, colors will not chip off, but will shrink, making it a fault difficult to remedy. A small quantity of oil of cloves added to the mixing medium will prevent blistering.

Blistering is a very common fault with decalcomania, or transfer work; and is caused by insufficient washing and drying of transfers, on their application. A very thin wash of oil of cloves, over the already dried transfer will be a good preventive. Dab it on with a slightly moistened pad, but above all, dry your transfers from any possible speck of water.

CHAPTER XX

THE GLAZING OF UNDERFIRED CHINA

Firing, even for the expert decorator, is frequently very perplexing. Often, having taken every precaution and attended to each particular in the usual manner, the artist will be surprised to take from the kiln pieces fired in a manner vastly different from what he expected.

Overfiring will destroy so much of the work, that, bearing this in mind, his most precious decorations are more apt to be underfired. In such a case it is not advisable to refire china without going over the work with a thin coat of color, and this may be as light as you please to make it.

Do not get the idea that the article needs a very strong firing. Fire it at the same heat which you ordinarily use to produce a good glaze.

If you should not wish to go over the entire decoration, cover the fired colors with a light coat of thin oil like enamel oil, oil of copaiba, or mixing oil and turpentine. Pad this coat well and let it dry thoroughly. Now dust this with white flux or ivory glaze, and the small amount of powder which will adhere to the oil will produce the desired glaze. Fire only at regular heat.

A coat of lustre, over underfired china will not produce a glaze. On the contrary, underfired colors will absorb the glazy substance of the lustre, changing the colors and probably resulting in a frosted effect.

White lustre over a very lightly fired tint may retain its glaze, but the result is always uncertain. We advise the artist to retouch the decoration and powder it with ivory glaze when colors are very dry, and this is undoubtedly the most reliable method.

Under no circumstances should the student apply pure glazes or fluxes mixed with oil over the unglazed decoration, as this, in most cases, will destroy the colors underneath. A light rubbing with the finest emery paper will improve a slightly rough surface.

The oil made by the overflowing of turpentine in your cup (where you wash the brushes) is a good glazing oil. The fluxes of the colors washed in it, produce its glazy qualities. See that this oil is clean and apply a light wash on the underfired decoration. Pat well, let dry and fire. You will notice the good glaze produced by it.

CHAPTER XXI
OXIDIZING OF COLORS

Different colors are manufactured with various metals as a basis; reds, browns, and flesh tints, for instance, are made with iron as a basis, while for yellow and greens, less iron is used in proportion.

Purples, carmines, roses, violets and pinks are made on a basis of gold and tin, and in mixing colors made upon different metal basis their effectiveness is altered.

Our experience is that, purple mixed with black or brown frequently loses its glaze and becomes oxidized, while the same purple mixed with a good dark green will stand a better chance of keeping its glaze. This is because greens have a smaller quantity of iron. The oxidizing is of course the result of the contact of the two different metals and cannot be easily remedied. The only possible help would be a scroll of gold or silver, which is so opaque that it will cover every fault.

It sometimes happens that a decorated vase comes from the firing with a perfect glaze, but gradually loses its brilliancy and becomes matt. In this case the color is heavy and not sufficiently fired. Being porous, it absorbs the humidity of the air and apparently becomes oxidized. This can easily be washed out with soap and water and must be well dried. It is better to refire the china to prevent a repetition of this fault.

Purples and browns acquire a dull unpleasant appearance when too much oil is used in mixing them. The student should be especially careful when such colors as these are being mixed and used. Keep them as dry as possible, and the danger of oxidizing will be reduced to a minimum.

CHAPTER XXII
PASTE OR RELIEF WORK FOR GOLD

The two greatest faults of paste decorations are the flattening of the strokes and the chipping off of the paste. Both of these faults may be traced to the misuse of oil,—using either the wrong quality or too large a quantity. Insufficient grinding of the paste will also result badly, and it is best to grind paste well with turpentine, and then let it dry before mixing it with oil. Either a horn or a steel knife will answer the purpose. Different artists have different ways of mixing paste, with, perhaps, the same good result, but professionals who do only the best work for English or French manufacturers mix their paste with two parts of fat oil and one part of oil of tar. Mix the paste on a ground glass slab to a sort of half-thick consistency, with the given proportion of oil, until it is perfectly smooth. Be especially careful to grind perfectly, according to these instructions.

The paste is now of the consistency of freshly mixed china colors. Stir it with a knife, and leaning over it, breathe (do not blow) upon it. Stir it again and again, until it has become hard and adheres to the knife in a stringy way. The most important points in this work is the reducing of the paste to the right consistency, so that when, in scooping it up just as one does with enamels, it will hang on to the paste brush and keep a good shape.

A small amount of water will answer the same purpose as the breathing, but it requires great care to get just the right quantity. Too much humidity will cause the paste to become stiff and bad. After having scooped up the paste, apply it either in scroll or dot forms with a firm stroke. A good paste line is made with a single long stroke; by going over the line, an uncertain and uneven appearance will result, which will affect the beauty of paste work. The stroke, to be good, must keep the high, round thickness of a cord. If it flattens, the paste is too oily; breathe upon it again to remedy this fault.

Paste must be frequently stirred and kept in a little heap while you are using it. In picking up the paste with your brush, always take it from the center of the heap, where it is apt to be more fresh. In remixing paste, use as little oil as possible, and it will be safest to have freshly mixed paste every day.

To straighten an imperfect line, use either a hard point or a brush slightly moistened with turpentine. Clean the brush whenever it has become clogged and refill it with fresh paste. A red sable brush is the best one to use for this work. Paste may be applied over fired colors or lustres as well as on white china. It must be well dried without artificial means, before firing. Gold should be applied after the paste is fired, to obtain the best results, though it is possible to apply it on unfired paste, providing the paste is perfectly dry; but the result will not be so satisfactory.

It is a very difficult matter to remedy chipped paste; the only possible way is to reapply it on the places where it is missing, and, in order to avoid an extra firing, apply the gold directly on the new paste (after it is dry) in the same firing.

Use unfluxed gold over paste; do not mix liquid bright gold with it and do not apply the latter over the paste alone, as it would injure the brilliancy of the burnish gold. Silver can also be applied over paste, two coats of burnish silver being generally necessary for the best results.

ADDITIONAL NOTES.—After the paste is fired, you can rub the gold in powder form over it, using your finger tip. The paste retains enough of the gold and make the gilding quick to accomplish.

NOTE 2.—One-eighth of white oxide of tin mixed with the paste will prevent the chipping off.

CHAPTER XXIII
SILVER

Silver is used in the same manner as gold. For a fine burnish silver effect, apply the liquid bright silver on first firing and burnish silver on the second, though two coats of burnish silver will result satisfactorily. Burnish silver works well over paste for gold relief, which must be fired before applying the silver. It may be necessary to apply the silver over paste in two firings, in order to obtain the natural brilliancy of the metal. Mix silver with turpentine or oil of lavender, if in paste form, and with fat oil if in powder form, in which case grind it well.

Silver applied near pink or rose colors, will affect them. By mixing one part of Roman gold with two parts of liquid bright silver, a fair imitation of platinum may be obtained. Two parts of Roman gold to one part of silver will produce green-gold,—the greater the quantity of silver the lighter will be the color of the gold. (See the chapters on Gold.) In fact, whenever Roman gold is of too strong a color, reduce it with a trifle of burnish silver.

Both burnish and liquid bright silver can be applied, separately or mixed, over fired colors or on white china. They can also be applied over gold, without affecting their appearance. Liquid bright silver, if too thin or if overfired, will have a milky appearance. In that case, reapply the same liquid, or, if desired, apply the burnish silver. (See recipe for Silver.)

ADDITIONAL NOTES—Some decorators mix the powder silver with 25% of liquid bright gold, and claim that this neutralizes the tarnishing, without changing the silver color.

NOTE 2.—The reason for the tarnishing of silver applied on china is that this metal absorbs the sulphur hydrogen and sulphur dioxide always present in the air, forming the grayish compound, obscuring the brilliancy of the metal.

CHAPTER XXIV
PADS AND DABBERS

Pads and dabbers are used extensively to facilitate the making of an even ground, or the flushing of one or of many different colors combined.

Pads can be made of silk, chamois skin, unstarched cheesecloth, or any similar material. The older and the more washed the piece of cloth, the smoother will be the work, and the better will be the results. A large wad of cotton or lamb's wool compressed into a little ball until nearly hard, and covered with either one of the aforesaid materials, will make a pad.

Tie the dabber on the back, so as to keep it stretched smoothly on the cotton, and also to prevent any wrinkles, which would spoil the ground. With a lighted match burn the lint which may be hanging from the face of the dabber, and proceed to pad the color in one quick, straight stroke. If you pad sideways, the color wiii be scratched off. Pad quickly and remove the pad with out pressing the dabber on the colors, working in a gentle hammering way, quick and light.

A silk dabber is the one mostly used, and an old handkerchief or any frequently washed piece of silk will do very nicely. We find also that a very fine piece of cheesecloth answers the purpose splendidly, especially on heavy grounds, where the silk is apt to retain too much of the color.

This cheesecloth, after the lint has been burned from it, will permit the oil to be absorbed by the cotton, and will not retain much of the tint. This method is used by all practical decorators of china and has proved successful and clean.

It is not advisable to pad a ground while the color is still very fresh, as a large part of the color would be taken up by the pad. By allowing a short time for setting, the color will remain and the work will be more satisfactory.

Stipples are frequently used to spread heavy coats of colors before beginning the dabbing with cloth, and this is undoubtedly the best method for obtaining good results.

When you notice that your pad produces an uneven, grainy effect, rub the pad on a clean piece of paper, for the purpose of removing the color hanging on the cloth, and proceed with the padding. It is advisable to wet your dabbers with a trifle of mixing oil before padding to insure a more even result. For yellow-brown, banding blue, pinks, and grays, apply oil in a larger quantity to your pad.

Good cotton (commercial or surgeon's cotton) or lamb's wool make a good material for the pads.

CHAPTER XXV
ACID ETCHING

Acid etching is the carving into the china itself, produced by the chemical action of hydrofluoric acid. It is best to do this work in the open air, so as not to inhale the fumes, and the student should wear rubber gloves to protect her hands.

After the design is sketched on the china, fill in the background with liquid asphalt or any other preparation sold in the shops for this purpose. Leave that part of the design which is to be etched absolutely clean and free of asphalt, in order to secure an even depth of

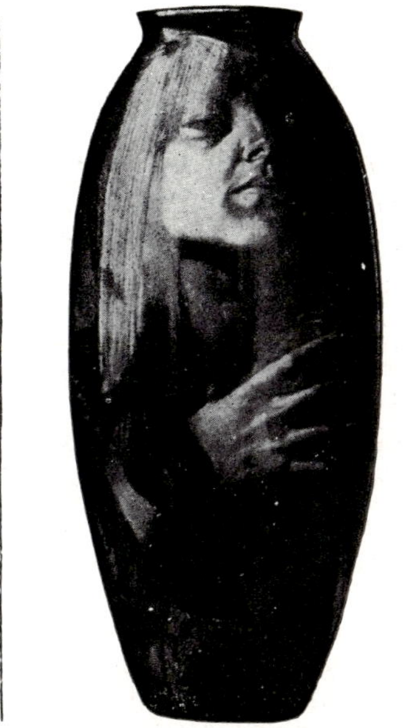

Figure No. 17

etching. The background properly covered will not be affected by the acid. Professional etchers dip the china into a large quantity of hydrofluoric acid and leave it in ten or fifteen minutes or more, according to the depth desired. The longer in the acid the deeper the etching. But amateurs, who have not the facilities of a professional, will find the following method quite satisfactory.

Put a small amount of any fine powder, such as flint, burnishing sand, spar, or white lead upon a useless bit of china and moisten it with hydrofluoric acid until it has the semi-liquid consistency of paste. Use a stick instead of a knife, as the acid will ruin the knife or anything else of value.

Apply enough of this paste over the clean design with a stick, until it has about the thickness of a five-cent (nickel) piece. Leave it undisturbed for half an hour or more, then wash away the acid with running water, being careful, of course, not to touch it with the hand. Now remove the asphalt with turpentine and clean the article thoroughly. A shallow unglazed design will show on the china, produced by the acid, which will have destroyed the china enamel.

The design will not appear deep, but is usually deep enough, and a deeper etching will result if acid is allowed to remain longer on the china.

If a good coat of gold is laid over both etched and unetched parts of the china, and fired, the gold will have a deep matt appearance over the etched parts and the regular brilliancy over the unetched surfaces, making a beautiful contrast of brilliant and matt golds. Gold should all be burnished.

The excellent effect of acid etching for plates and flat pieces will sufficiently repay the artist for all his

ADDITIONAL NOTE.—By applying acid varnish, or asphalt with a sponge, in a rough way, sponging the china, a pretty all over, hammered effect will be made when etched china will be covered with gold.

anxiety and trouble. It is advisable to apply two coats of pure gold.

We wish to lay special stress upon the danger of handling the acid. It requires the greatest care, and should a drop of it come in contact with the skin or clothes, wash at once with soda water and apply vaseline or bread soaked in milk to relieve the skin. For burns, hold the finger in tincture of Spanish flies. Keep the bottle of acid well closed, as the evaporation is apt to destroy any kind of materials, without mentioning your china decorations.

CHAPTER XXVI
AGATE ETCHING

Agate etching is the engraving made with agate on the already fired Roman gold. The best gold background for this work is made by applying a generous coat of liquid bright gold on the china; while this is still wet, dust the powdered Roman gold over it. When this is fired and burnished, the gold will have a satin half-matt appearance. The engraving with the pointed agate can be done at this stage, but it would insure better success to draw the design or monogram with pure Roman gold and refire. The gold should not be burnished, and the etching should be made over this second gold drawing of the monogram or design.

Use the agate (which should be pointed) as you would use a pencil, pressing the point on the gold and endeavoring to produce a clean long line. The student

See imitation etchings on page 135.

should remember that the real beauty of agate etchings depends on the beauty of the lines.

Any design to be etched can be transferred over the gold by using graphite paper. In etching a monogram it is necessary to be very sure of the letters that compose it, to eliminate every possibility of a mistake which could not be easily remedied.

The gold background is now half-matt, and the etching should appear strong and brilliant, much like the drawing of a needle on a brass surface. Do not re-fire the gold after etching, as that would destroy the work, and it would have to be repeated after the next firing.

Etchings can also be made upon a generous coat of Roman gold alone, applied in the usual manner with a brush. Fire and burnish it, and proceed to apply the monogram in gold alone, as explained in the previous method. It is now to be fired, but the gold is not to be burnished this time, and begin the etching.

As it would detract from the effectiveness of the etching to produce too glossy a background, it would not be advisable to use liquid bright gold for this part of the work, as this metal is naturally very brilliant.

CHAPTER XXVII
BANDING

Banding and lining, like paste work in china, requires practice and a steady hand.

A good band is generally obtained if the banding wheel is used.

The china is to be placed in the center of the disk, and a number of lines engraved on this disk itself, will assist in finding its perfect center.

Spin the banding wheel and rest your arm on a table or some other firm support, so as to keep the brush in a steady position, touching the china lightly. In other words, instead of moving the brush around the china, let the china move around the brush and touch it lightly.

In turning the wheel, be careful to avoid too swift a motion, as it will cause the china to fall or to slip away from the smooth surface of the disk. A few small pieces of wax used to fasten the china to the disk, may help to keep the china in the right place.

To make a small line, use a thin brush, but a broader one is necessary to make a band.

Do not use the colors too hard or too dry, but keep them in a half-liquid state, so that they will flow easily and produce an even line. Let the brush run over the same line repeatedly.

Bands are made in gold and silver, as well as in color, and can also be made with grounding oil, for the purpose of dusting with powder, as in the groundlaying process.

This method gives better result than wet colors, for a broad band, as the band will be even and glazy. For lines or edges, a long deer-footed liner is used, this brush being more desirable on account of its capacity for the quantity of color needed in the long round line.

Lines should be made in one long stroke; many and

Note.—Good lines can be made with a compass, having a ruling pen, filled with china color, made liquid with diluting medium. Use it as a compass, or the lines can also be drawn around smooth edges of saucers, bowls, etc.

short strokes will make imperfect lines. Gold and silver lines are made in the same way, but for this purpose those metals should be more liquid than the usual painting consistency.

CHAPTER XXVIII
GOLD AND SILVER BURNISHING

When Roman gold comes from the kiln, its appearance is matt, and a rubbing or burnishing is necessary to bring out its natural brilliancy. The most practical, though not the best way, is to rub the fired gold with a spun glass brush, especially made for this work. Rub the gold heavily and evenly until its proper color is obtained. Clean the china very thoroughly of the glass fibers. If the china should be refired before cleaning, the molten glass fibers would destroy the decorations. Glass fibres will have the same pernicious effect if blown or mixed in any way with fresh colors, either on the palette or on the china.

Burnish the gold every time before handling the china or reapplying the gold. Unburnished gold will absorb the perspiration of the fingers, and that will, of course, affect the beauty of the metal.

Burnishing sand is often used for rubbing, especially in parts that cannot be reached by the brush. For this purpose, moisten with water a piece of soft cloth, dip it into the sand, taking up all that will adhere to it, and rub the gold lightly. When the gold is well polished, wash the china with water. If gold rubs off in burnishing, it is underfired, and must be reapplied and refired.

Agate or bloodstone burnishing gives the best appearance to gold. Designs may be traced on unburnished gold with an agate tracer, but for this it is best to have a powdered gold ground; this will give a softer appearance to the gold.

Silver is burnished in the same manner as gold. By applying a coat of liquid bright gold on first firing, and Roman gold on the second, the gold will be burnished easier and more evenly. Glass brush burnishing, is the quickest and most practical, but agate or bloodstone burnishing will give a higher polish to the gold; and gold, especially on table ware, will wear much longer when burnished with agate or bloodstone.

CHAPTER XXIX
CUTTING OUT

It is often necessary to cut out a design from a background, either dry or wet, and to this purpose we would make the following suggestions.

The design to be cut out from the background should be visible through the background itself, and to produce this, we give more information in the chapter on outlining. The outlining of the design is generally done with china ink for wet grounds, and to make this design visible through a solid dusted ground, outline it with a pointed stick over the already padded oil and before applying the powdered colors. The stick will act as a scratcher on the oil, and the powder applied afterward will not adhere there for lack of moisture, showing a light trace of the full design on the ground. distinct enough to indicate its meaning. On a wet ground or a ground applied with a brush, the drawing will generally show through.

Let us return to dry grounds. It takes about twenty-four hours for the dusted colors to dry naturally, but artificial heat may hasten the process. If the design appears sufficiently clear, apply over the parts to be cut out a light coat of oil of cloves mixed with a few shavings of soap. Use sparingly to prevent it from running beyond your lines. The mixture will soften the dry colors in about five minutes. Now, with a piece of cotton fastened to your finger tip, remove the oil of cloves with a firm stroke, and the design will show clean and clearly.

Remember that if the ground is still wet, the oil of cloves will spread beyond the space for which it is intended and will spoil the sharpness of the lines. Also be careful in rubbing off the oil of cloves, not to draw the cotton outside of the design to be cut out, which is apt to happen if you wipe the color outward with the cotton. Wipe from the edges toward the inside. Keep changing the cotton so as to have it fresh and clean for every little bit of oil that you remove.

Of course, a design can be cut out from a dry ground with a stick without the use of oil of cloves, but it should be done very carefully while the ground is fresh. The former method, however, is the one most frequently used and will give very satisfactory results; tar oil is also used instead of oil of cloves.

To cut out a design from a wet tinted ground while the color is still fresh, use a brush kept clean with turpentine, but use it almost dry. Diluting medium is a very good substitute for turpentine; it is really more reliable and will not spread as turpentine often does.

Another method of cutting out used by practical decorators, and very useful when such work is done on a large scale, is the following: Add as much molasses to lampblack as you would add oil to ordinary china colors. Add a few drops of water, and mix it all thoroughly. Apply this with a clean brush, so as to cover all of the design to be cut out, to the thickness of a twenty-five cent piece. Dry it well and proceed to groundlay, in the regular way, first with oil, then with powder, covering the entire piece of china, design and all.

Allow about six hours for drying, and then dip your article into lukewarm water, paying special attention to having the design deep in the water. This will not affect the ground in the least. In a short time, according to the temperature of the water, you will notice a raising of the design, and this will begin to peel off. When you see the design raised in every part, wipe it off with a clean piece of cotton moistened with water. The design can now be painted if desired. This method of cutting out is mostly used in large establishments where china and glass for commercial use is decorated in large quantities, and it gives very satisfactory results.

CHAPTER XXX
COLOR COMBINATIONS

Good taste for color in dressing, a good combination of veils, flowers, and ribbons, denotes a certain education in the wearer, and we must concede that ladies are superior to men in this special gift of color selection.

The writer, in planning a novel scheme of colors, very often wanders among millinery displays and studies their splendid combination of colors, their delicate tints and contrasts, which, when applied to decorations of china, make equally beautiful effects. It would appear, therefore, that ladies having a better opportunity to see, wear and decide among such a variety of pretty combinations, should make excellent colorists in the different branches of painting. A good design is often ruined by a bad combination of colors. A border of dark finishing brown, for instance, will look well with almost all colors, though not always with blue or green. Clear blue tints, as a rule, give a disagreeable effect, with the exception of Copenhagen blue and the dark blackish blues. But to keep to the browns, a very harmonious effect is produced by a combination of finishing brown, yellow brown, and ivory yellow, adding, if de-

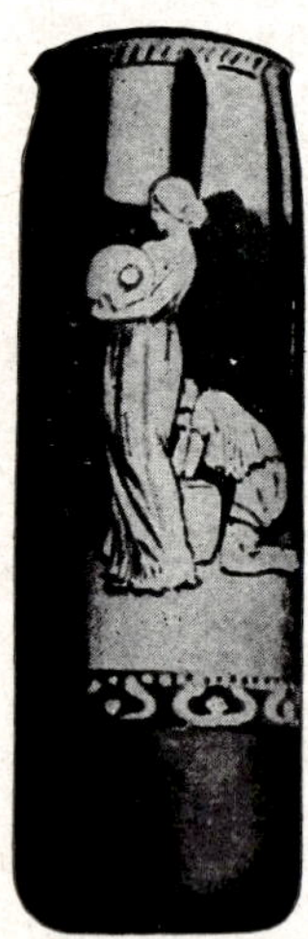

Figure No. 18

sired, a touch of gold. Violet of iron and auburn brown, on a grayish ground, combine well. Copenhagen blue and pearl gray produce a very soft pretty effect. Violet color looks well with grayish tones and with ivory and light yellow-green tints. A vase in yellow tones, with daffodils, yellow roses, or some conventional motif, might have a background of pale yellow and a gold scroll worked into it; and the effect would be very strong, but good. As a rule, however, yellows are not very useful in producing delicate color combinations.

Peacock and sultan green are very good for Turkish effects. For this style of work, black, red, and dark brown, with a touch of yellow, green, and blue, will be appropriate. Olive green, Copenhagen blue, new green, violet of iron, and auburn brown, applied alone, make very soft, pleasing backgrounds. A heavy border of Copenhagen blue painted with gold designs is very good.

Dark Mazarine blue cannot be procured for general over-glaze decoration, but banding blue, mixed with about one-fifth of hair black, will make a fine dark blue. A silver design looks well over dark greens or dark grays.

Blues and blue greens do not combine well with reds; neither do rose color and red. Red and olive green combined look well. Red and black make a strong contrast, as do also black or dark green, and yellow green. A dark green band will harmonize well with ivory yellow, or light green. A maroon band looks well with over-designs in gold. A good strong maroon can be made by mixing ruby purple with one-sixth of peacock green.

A good dark gray is made by mixing Copenhagen blue with one quarter of Russian green. Under no circumstances should yellow and red be mixed together, as the yellows, being naturally fluxy, would destroy the red. Rose color and pink look best when combined with light yellow green, or bluish greens, or grays. Purple and ruby also look well when near light greens and grays.

Violet and yellow brown, if put together, will have a very striking effect. Tan color can be made with a light wash of Meissen, or hair brown. A delicate bluish gray is made with turquoise blue and one-sixth or even less of black, according to the depth of color desired. A deep, warm effect is produced by a dark green ground, which, on next firing, is covered with crimson purple or ruby. Another beautiful color will be obtained, if three parts of peacock green are mixed with one part of crimson purple, to produce a deep steel blue. By changing these proportions, other equally good tints may be obtained.

CHAPTER XXXI
SLOW OR QUICK DRYING OF COLORS

It happens frequently that the student is hampered in his efforts to produce a certain effect by the drying of colors. Sometimes they do not dry quickly enough, and other times it is desirable to have them dry more slowly. In working up some designs or in painting a broad ground, it is often necessary to have slow drying colors. For this purpose add a drop or so of oil of cloves in mixing the colors. The greater the amount of this oil added, the longer the colors will remain moist; but too much of it will cause the colors to run. Good judgment is a very necessary item.

Sweet oil will also keep the colors open, though even less of this is to be used than of the oil of cloves, as too much of it will prevent the drying of the colors for several days.

We use the regular mixing medium with the colors, and to keep the colors moist while working we use the diluting medium. Many artists use mixing oil or oil of lavender, but we find that the first is too thick and the second dries too quickly, while the diluting medium as a working oil, is very smooth and allows the artist sufficient time to carry out a design or ground before drying. The diluting medium could be mixed with the color at first, but as it is always necessary to have some sort of liquid to moisten the brush in working, it will be desirable to use this oil then, and in the proportions desired. Use it sparingly, however, as too much of it will cause the colors to run, and by using this, it will not be necessary to add either oil of cloves or sweet-oil in mixing the colors. If it is desirable to have the colors dry quickly, add a small quantity of turpentine or oil of lavender to the colors; the former being the most effective. By mixing your colors with mixing oil and when properly mixed, adding a few drops of turpentine and remixing them, the drying will be quick and thorough. For drying or rather stopping of running colors, breathe on them (do not blow) repeatedly, and the humidity of your breath will clog and stop them without affecting their properties. On the same principle, steam from hot water will work successfully.

CHAPTER XXXII
UNDERGLAZE EFFECTS

Real underglaze effects are painted either under or over the china enamel, and for this purpose special strong colors and high temperature in firing are absolutely necessary. Specially built kilns are required, on account of the strong heat given for the melting of the colors and glaze.

Few colors will stand such firing, and real underglaze effects should not be attempted with a regular china kiln. The most essential quality of underglaze decoration is the strong even coat of glaze, covering the entire surface, and also the softness of every line. Some colors give a delicate blurred effect, making a very beautiful blended tone.

To produce a good imitation of underglaze effects with vitrifiable china colors, the article must be carefully dusted with glazes or fluxes at every firing.

Paint the china in the usual way, and, when very dry, dust the entire decoration with a good soft glaze, blowing off carefully every bit of superficial powder; fire at regular heat. Repeat the firing and repeat the dusting; the oftener the china is fired the stronger will be the glaze.

To produce the desired softness of the lines apply a little powdered colors on the outer edge of the decoration. It must be done with a very dry, small brush, much in the same way as painting is done. Take special pains to apply this powder color very evenly all along the lines, and blend it very carefully.

This powdered color can be applied either before or after the general dusting. It must be remembered that red and flesh tones are easily affected by fluxes and glazes, and therefore should be covered as little as possible, or perhaps left entirely untouched. The repeated dusting of glazes and the blending of all sharp lines will produce a good imitation of underglaze decorations.

There are tinted glazes like pink, blue, green, and lavender glazes, by the use of which, instead of white glaze, a delicate tinted surface may be attained.

Do not attempt to dust too thick a coat of glaze for one firing, as this is apt to give a speckled appearance to the colors, but apply sparingly and attempt to produce the desired effect by a succession of light dustings and firings.

CHAPTER XXXIII
ERASING

To erase fired colors, use the china eraser, which is a composition made up of hydrofluoric and nitric acids. If possible wear rubber gloves in using it.

Pure hydrofluoric acid is being extensively used for

this purpose, but it is dangerous to the china as well as to the artist. It is so powerful an acid that, besides erasing the color it often sinks into the china and destroys its enamel.

Much excruciating pain has been endured by the unfortunate artists who have used it carelessly and touched it with their hands. The china eraser on the contrary is comparatively mild and may be washed off the hands, though extra care should be taken to avoid contact with it. Handle it directly from the bottle with a stick and apply it to the parts to be erased, taking special care not to go over any other part of the decoration. Rub the parts repeatedly with the stick and apply it twice if necessary until the color has disappeared. Wash the china with clear water and dry it well.

Heavy colors, of course, require longer erasing in proportion to their depth. Burnish gold and silver require long rubbing, while liquid bright gold and silver, as well as lustres, erase very easily. The china can be repainted with very good results after this erasing. If you wish to erase a mark in a very particular design without danger to the rest of the work near it, lay a broad line of liquid asphalt or wax around the mark, very carefully, leaving the part to be erased absolutely clean.

Apply the eraser, which will be kept in bounds by the asphalt or wax, and the rest of the work will be safe from injury. When the artist through inexperience or carelessness burns his hands with hydrofluoric acid or the eraser, an incision is usually made and a liquid composed of Spanish flies and laudanam is applied to the affected part. Always handle the stick from the same end to prevent trouble.

CHAPTER XXXIV
PLATINUM

Platinum is sold in paste or powder form and is used like burnish gold or silver. Its appearance is somewhat like silver, but more subdued and grayish in tone. It is very often preferable to silver for its wearing qualities and for the fact that its glaze does not tarnish. One good coat of platinum will stand successive firings without losing its strength. Platinum can be used in gold work and makes a very pretty combination when used with red gold and green gold. Liquid bright platinum is used much like liquid bright gold. A fair imitation of platinum can be obtained by mixing one part of Roman gold to two parts of liquid bright silver.

CHAPTER XXXV
BRONZES

Burnish bronzes are generally bought in powder form and can be obtained in various colors, green bronze, yellow bronze, red bronze, etc. These tints are used to produce old Roman or Grecian bronze effects and make peculiar combinations.

In mixing bronze powder with oil, do not grind too heavily, as the little particles of gold that produce the bronze effect would disappear in the grinding. Burnish lightly with a glass brush or sand. Bronzes should be applied thickly but smoothly. Mix them with fat oil and proceed with them in the same manner as with gold. Gold bronzes can be made by adding a trifle of matt color to the gold paste. Do not grind too much.

CHAPTER XXXVI
APPLICATION OF DECALCOMANIAS OR TRANSFERS

Designs of different subjects like flowers, fruit, figures, and trade-mark stamps, are painted on paper with china colors by a special process and then transferred to the china or glass to be fired. These designs are called decalcomanias or, more commonly, transfers.

There are several methods of making these transfers, and the methods of applying them differ accordingly. There are the film transfers which are applied face up. Moisten them in hot water until the film covering one side of the paper begins to peel off. Then place your paper on the china, picture facing upward, and begin to pull the paper from under the film, so that this latter, which holds the design, will stay and stick on the china. It is also possible to detach the moistened film very carefully with the palette knife and apply it to the china. In any case, a good bath of hot water (not boiling) to make the film very pliable, is necessary. If the film should wrinkle in the taking off of the paper, stretch carefully and dry well before firing. The white film surrounding the design will disappear in the fire.

Other decalomanias are applied face downward. Give these pictures a light coat of a special transfer varnish, and when this latter becomes tacky, lay the picture downward on a moistened piece of cloth or chamois and dampen its back with cold water to make the paper more pliable. Now apply the picture facing the china and rub it down with a roller, always rolling from the center. Wet well with a sponge and water and carefully remove the paper. In case of any wrinkle appearing on the transfer, press and stretch it with damp cloth or chamois skin.

There are other makes of transfer which do not need the light coat of varnish. These are simply bathed thoroughly in cold water for fifteen minutes or longer, applied on china and bathed well on the back with sponge and water. Leave them undisturbed for about fifteen minutes and remove the paper.

The student should always remember to dry the transfer perfectly well, after paper is removed, as any blistering in the firing is caused by the tacky liquid holding the transfer on the paper, and this must be dried off well. Decalcomania trade-mark stamps, are applied by the same method. The tinting or retouching of transfers should properly be done on the second firing, though light touches around the designs can be applied on the first fire with the film. The tinting is painted or padded and even dusted in the same manner as regular hand painting effects are done.

Note.—If the transfer varnish becomes thick with time, add a trifle of turpentine and shake well.

CHAPTER XXXVII
JEWELED WORK

A number of glass jewels are made for ceramic use to imitate the topaz, turquoise, sapphire, pearl, ruby, and emerald. These jewels withstand regular firing without melting or losing their brilliancy and are to be applied as follows: Mix the jewel cement with water until of medium consistency. Apply it in the place intended for the jewel, using more or less according to its size. Pick up the jewel with a brush moistened with water and lay it on the cement, pressing lightly. The cement will hold the jewel and should be thoroughly dry before being fired.

A light or Belleek firing is advisable for this work, and if fired with other china, the jeweled pieces should be placed in the front part of the kiln. It is dangerous to fire them more than once, and if they come off, there is nothing to be done except to scrape off the cement and reapply as before, though cold cement, not to be fired, may help in an emergency.

Jewels are also imitated by applying tinted enamels in the form of jewels, or by using white enamel and tinting it on successive firing.

For instruction in the use of enamels, see the chapter under that heading.

CHAPTER XXXVIII
KILN REPAIRING

The frequent firing and strong heat makes it necessary to replace or repair the different parts composing a kiln. The heavy stacks of china will often crack or damage the bottom tiles of a revelation kiln, and the heat will in time damage the walls. It is advisable for the artist to have at hand some fire clay, which can be bought in powder and moistened with water. Handle it and make it pliable and of the thickness of putty, possibly not quite so thick.

Apply it all along the crack, taking special care to fill the cavity only. Superfluous clay only helps to make scales and dust. In replacing the bottom tiles, use this clay where they join. For the replacing of the tubes on the wall, the top of the kiln may be lifted, but in such a case the manufacturer of the kiln is willing to give full instructions on the matter. In a kiln with iron pot, cracks can be filled with fire clay, and, if necessary, with a band of asbestos cloth on the outside. On this kiln a whitewash with kiln enamel every few months will help in producing better results in the decorating. Attempt to keep your kiln in good repair and clean, as this will undoubtedly contribute in giving a satisfactory glaze to your china.

CHAPTER XXXIX
OPAQUE GLASS PAINTING

Opaque glass is the white glass used in manufacturing lamp globes, perfume bottles, pepper and salt shakers, vases, and many different white glass articles. This glass is generally heavier than the transparent table glass and will require a stronger fire than this latter, but will not need the degree of heat given to china. To obtain a good result glass should be fired separately from china, as the heat required by one would be unsatisfactory for the other.

Paint opaque glass with regular, already mixed glass colors, which can be bought at reasonable prices, or use the regular china color mixed with glass flux in different proportions according to their properties. For instance, add one-third of glass flux to two-thirds of color for the blues, greens, and grays; one-fourth of glass flux to three-quarter of color for the browns and blacks; one-sixth of glass flux to five-sixths of color for the reds and yellows. For the purples, pinks, roses and violets (but not for the violet of iron), use a special flux for pinks, which is composed on a different basis and is made purposely for these colors. A good medium for glass painting is made of balsam of copaiba (this should be of fresh quality) mixed with one-twentieth of oil of cloves and about as much sweet-oil. The oil of cloves will prevent blistering, while the sweet-oil will help the decorator in keeping the colors soft and smooth. The difficulty of painting on opaque glass, and especially on lamp globes, is the smoothness of the stroke. Should one stroke be heavy and the other light, the color be lumpy and grainy, or should the oil run, all these faults, which may not show on china, will appear strongly when the artificial light is placed inside the globe. Then, through the light, everything will show, and if the color is misapplied, the effect will be very bad. It is advisable to paint such glass in front of or near the window so that any possible mistake may be seen through the glass, while working. Colors on glass can be padded, ground-laid, or dusted according to the method used on china. Mediums used for china painting can be safely used for painting on glass. The firing for this glass must be very light, and it is safe to say that when your kiln begins to become red all over, the fire must be closed off. If your fire goes too far and becomes lighter than a dark cherry color, your glass will melt, lose its shape and be lost.

It is a common occurrence to have a large piece of glass fired well on one side and not enough on the other. This happens when glass is fired in a small kiln, which generally has a stronger heat at the back and a lighter fire in front. To prevent this, dust lightly with glass flux the part of the glass that will face toward the front of the kiln, and leave the part facing the back without flux. This will help in making an even glaze.

Also, if possible, to prevent heating too strongly on the side, where kiln walls come near to the glass, protect the walls with asbestos board or tiles. Glass can be fired several times. For glass use unfluxed gold in case any gold is wanted. Liquid bright gold works very well. Enamels do not chip off even if thickly applied.

CHAPTER XL
TURPENTINE

Brushes are cleansed with turpentine. There is a considerable number of students unable to stand its strong odor and to these we would advise the use of a lighter oil like lavender oil or diluting medium or also a strong solution of soap and water. When this latter is used, the brush should be well dried before taking of the color for the decorations. Only a small quantity of the lavender oil is necessary if this is used. Put the brush into the oil and press the colors out on a cloth with your fingers. Do not rinse. Spirits is very good for washing lustre and gold brushes.

CHAPTER XLI

COLORS

In order to enlighten the student in the relation of the tints with their respective names, we will write a list of the most popular and useful colors, listed from the lightest to the very darkest of their individual class. Ivory yellow is the lightest of the yellows, primrose is a trifle darker, lemon is next, albert yellow, deep yellow, egg yellow and the darkest is orange yellow. Under blues come baby blue, turquoise blue, sevres blue, air blue, banding blue, copenhagen blue, royal blue and aztec blue. Under the green, light water green, apple green, gray green, yellow green, moss green, deep blue green, olive green, brown green, russian green, persian green, peacock green, sultan green, royal green, shading green, new green, empire green, myrtle green and darkest green. Under the browns—imperial ivory, yellow ochre, yellow brown, meissen brown, auburn brown, hair brown, chestnut brown, finishing brown. Under the reds—Carnation, yellow red, light pompadour, blood red, dark pompadour, violet of iron. Under the pinks—Rose salmon, rose color, peach blossom, american beauty, ruby purple, crimson purple, violet color, deep violet of gold, royal purple. Under grays—Lavender glaze, pearl gray, copenhagen gray, ashes of roses, and the following: purple black, best black and hair black.

CHAPTER XLII

BRUSHES

Flat, quill camel hair brushes are the brushes generally used for china decoration. They are called *square shaders,* or if round, *pointed shaders.* They vary in size from a few hairs to about one-half inch broad. These are used for all applications of moist colors.

Tinting brushes are used for broader surfaces and are also made of camel's hair, but they have ferrule binding. They vary from three-eighths of an inch to one inch and even larger. Paste and enamel decorations require a stiffer brush, called *red sable.* They are long and pointed and come in different sizes. These red sable brushes are also used for small outlinings, although for this purpose, quill liners (which are sometimes called *miniature brushes* or *outliners*), are equally as good and are lower in price. They come in several small sizes.

Stipplers are used to blend one or more colors so as to make an even tint. They are used in a hammering way, blending out marks or edges, and are generally in quills, flat at the top. There is one kind of stippler that has a straight top and one with a slant top, these latter are called *deer foot* stipplers. Both kind vary from a few hairs to one inch or more in size. They are used much the same as a dabber and many decorators use stipplers at first and dabbers afterwards, attaining a very smooth effect.

Badger blenders are brushes used to dust powder colors on the china as explained in the chapter on dusting. Dry cotton is also used for this purpose. The size of the badger blenders varies from one-third to one and a half inches broad or more. In drying the brushes, while you work, be very careful not to pull the hairs, because this loosens and pulls them out. Brushes shed their hair when left to dry unclean and full of colors, in which case they become brittle. Moths or poor mountings in the quill are also causes for quick destruction of the brushes. A new brush will shed a few hairs at the beginning, but will become good when these loose hairs are discarded.

Clean the brushes with clear turpentine and in laying them away, see that they have a straight, natural shape. A good way to dry a brush is to press it on a piece of blotting paper or a cloth that is not wooly or full of lint. See that the hairs are not cramped when dried, for this makes them unfit for use.

CHAPTER XLIII
EFFECTS IN ONE-FIRING

It appears to be an impossibility to produce a good, complete decoration in one-firing, but very many effects can be made and are continually made, especially by large concerns and factories bound to economize in time, handling and any possible way. Lustre lends a good field in this line for the reason that a good ground or band is easily made in one-firing, especially with the mother of pearl, yellow pearl, green pearl, brilliant green, yellow and light green. To this may be added a design in color or gold, provided the space for this latter be carefully left clear on the china. In any case allow the lustres a thorough drying before the filling in of your design, and in applying the said design, avoid meddling with the lustres, even when they are dry.

In the chapter on lustre, several hints are given on trouble arising from bad lustre applications. Another good design may be made by a solid band of gold (Roman or unfluxed), and when this is dried a delicate design in silver applied over it. The other part of the china may be tinted in ivory yellow and a light design, in running succession, in dark green, or olive green, painted above and below the band (over the ivory yellow background). All this work can be easily made in one-firing and will look very delicate and complete. Other decorations can be made with general dusted ground of either regular colors or matt colors, similar to those advised for lustre effects. The dry ground having been applied (wet grounds are possible but not always successful), the designs can be cut out in white and the different subjects filled in. Lines or edges of gold can now be applied. When the whole is dried, the designs can be outlined with a dark color and everything will be complete. Of course many designs can be made in flat outlined work by sketching the full subject with china ink, after which you fill in the different parts with the various tints, and when dry, the outlines are applied with china colors. In these effects, a touch of lustre and gold intermixed with the regular powder color enhance the effect and make it look more elaborate. To give a fair illustration of the possibility of one-firing effect, the decorator should look at the variety of low-priced, commercial wares sold in the large crockery stores. Naturally, the correctness of those designs and the artistic quality of those articles are not very inspiring, but the number of different colors and intermixing of gold, lustre, etc., as found on them, seems a very difficult undertaking for one-firing, but such is not the fact for the attentive worker. Realistic subjects as flowers, fruit and landscapes can be made in one-firing. Apply at first the background, then your flowers and leaves, always remembering that some of the color disappears in the firing. When this decoration is dry, retouch carefully with more color and a small brush, applying much detail. Let this dry and then dust your decoration with different powder colors, blending in the subject with the background. The writer has often made the decoration given in this chapter and knows that the task is not a very difficult one, but simply a matter of careful application, and good handling. The above suggestions of one-firing effects, are only a few of the many different quickly-made decorations.

CHAPTER XLIV
STAMPING

Here is a relatively new method of decorating that may develop into something practical and in a number of different ideas. At present its artistic value is very limited, it having been exploited only for a certain grade of commercial ware, but its possibilities are much larger, and as stated above, may grow into something better. The idea is based on the rubber stamping work similar to any stamping done for dating or signing a letter, etc. Only in our case, instead of letters, ornaments and designs are placed on the stamps, which design being stamped in succession around the edge of a plate or cup, etc., produce a neat little border.

Up to the present time stamping borders of this kind have been made only in liquid bright gold, giving a rather common appearance to the china, but the writer has made many experiments with color stamping, and with good results. In fact, some of the works were very attractive.

The little designs are bought at reasonable prices either in loose sheets or mounted on a pliable piece of rubber. If they were mounted on wooden stumps, the design could not well adapt itself to the convex shape of the china, therefore the rubber mounting is preferred. The decorations giving very pretty effects are those in which the stamping is done with medium, a mixing oil rather thick and powder colors dusted over it.

The stamping must be done always with the same strength and with the same sparing quantity of oil so as to avoid one stamp to look darker than the other, which fault is very easily incurred.

Let us take a plate for instance and stamp an appropriate little design in oil all around the border. About fifteen minutes later dust this oil with either pearl gray or Copenhagen gray, light water green or any neutral light tint, and your border will appear at once. This being fired, a general light tint given all over the plate, border and all, and then again fired, the decorations will look simple but delicate and artistic. It is a difficult matter to stamp with Roman gold, and this can only be made by mixing a trifle of powdered gold with the stippling liquid bright gold. This latter is a special liquid bright gold, which is much thicker than the regular brand. Another way of using the stamps is with acid, applied over a solid ground or even on the white china. This acid will etch in the china and leave a clear design to be covered with gold or color.

In the chapter on acid etching, the effect is well explained and also the danger incurred by the misuse of the acid.

In conclusion, the stamping method is worth while knowing, not only for decorations but for trade-marks, signatures, monograms, etc.

CHAPTER XLV
LINT

When you paint on china you will always find more or less lint on the decorations, and this can only be avoided by being careful. Lint can be in the air, in the china, in the oil or in the brush itself. If the decorators will learn to mix the colors not too oily, in fact nearly thick, and use them as dry as possible, there will be no lint. It may fall on the decorations but there will be no oil to gather around it and it will produce no blemish, or mark. The air generally contains dust, which though not seen, will mix with oils and colors. This dust will not have the means to swell when the oil is very little. However, lint of this kind could be singed off the decoration with a match. Do this as quickly as possible so as not to warm the china. If this singing produces a smoky spot on the decoration this will disappear in the firing without injury to the decorations. Hair shedding brushes also cause some trouble. Scoop up the hair with a flat, barely moist brush. It can also be singed off or can be picked up carefully with a well pointed china wax-pencil. Press the point of the pencil on the hair and it will be picked up. Roughly ground colors always give grainy, poor effects and so much more when the colors are too oily. You often find small black specks on the fired china; this is generally caused by dust, fallen in the kiln or on the china before the firing. However, the china itself, when of poor surface, is apt to show some black blemishes. To avoid lint always singe the pads before you begin to decorate. You can always take away some of the lint or dust when the decorations are thoroughly dry, by scratching them off very carefully with a pocketknife or a steel eraser.

CHAPTER XLVI
FLUX

Flux, as mentioned in several chapters of this book, is a calcined lead, purified and finely ground. There are different natures of flux, hard, medium and soft, and also more or less good in qualities. It is used for the purpose of producing gloss and is generally mixed with colors and gold. The decorator's colors for china are nearly always sold with the proper quantity of flux already ground in them. The colors for glass decorations require fluxes as given in chapter on *Opaque Glass Painting*. In most cases gold also requires flux, as given in chapter on gold. Another function of the fluxes in their application to colors, etc., is the adherence they give to the china itself when they melt in the process of firing and prevent the colors from rubbing off.

CHAPTER XLVII
MIXING OF THE CHINA COLORS
(Chapter for the beginner)

The student begining to learn porcelain painting should be reminded of the necessity of having clean tools and finely mixed colors before undertaking any work.

Smooth colors, accelerate the work and produce perfect decorations. Gritty and badly ground colors save time but give a dusty looking, chipping china, producing decorations bound to adorn a very dark corner under the table.

Put on your clean white slab a small quantity of powder color, pour on it enough mixing medium to make a thick paste and amalgamate the two with a small palette knife, in a grinding way, so as to break up the rough particles of the color. It is better to have a small saucer with some of the mixing medium and take from this with the knife, rather than pouring the medium on the color with the bottle. In grinding with your knife, keep this latter well flat, without bending it too much, less it breaks, and mix forcibly until the color is a smooth, compact paste. Then put it on one side of the palette, clean what is left with a cloth, proceed to grind another color and having made this smooth, place it next to the first and so on until all the necessary tints are prepared. The student will find that some of the colors are quickly ground, while others require more time on account of their stony nature, but be patient and start well. Having now a cup of clean turpentine at hand and a small saucer with a few drops of a light working medium (diluting medium is very good in this case), take the color desired with a clean square brush, rubbing this down on the palette so as to have all the hair of the brush moist with it, and apply it on the china. It is understood that before applying the color, the student should carefully draw his design on the china, either with a wax pencil or china ink, which drawing will completely disappear in the firing. In fact, with the mixing of the colors, the correct drawing of the design is of utmost importance, because it leads the decorator to apply the tints in the proper place. If the colors seem to be too thick in working, take a trifle of the diluting medium with the brush and stir up the tinted brush on the palette. When changing colors, wash your brush in the turpentine and press the turpentine out before you dip it in another color, as turpentine evaporates and makes the colors thick.

As the writer does not know what decorations the different students may undertake, it will not be possible to say here which are the proper colors required. Make it a rule to apply the colors very even, using the brush in a flat way, and do not hesitate to clean away the design and repaint the china, if this does not look quite satisfactory. You may not like to do so at present, but will find the good result in the end. When the sitting is finished, always clean your palette and your brushes, these latter becoming hard and brittle when left to dry uncleaned.

We give in special chapters many suggestions on brushes, lining, tinting, oils, etc., which with this first lesson will help the beginner to the proper path.

The beginner will also learn that blue and purple or blue and ruby when mixed make violet. Blue and yellow produce green, green and a trifle of black make grav, reds (purples, rubies and pinks not included) mixed with black, make brown, etc. Do not mix the lustre colors, as these special liquids do not give good results when mixed in a raw state.

CHAPTER XLVIII
LIQUID BRIGHT GOLD

Liquid bright gold is a diluted solution of pure gold. It is used in combination with the Roman gold so as to economize, and also to give this latter a stronger adherence to the china enamel. It is used pure for commercial gilding on crockery and glass. Its appearance (when used alone) is bright and gaudy and it is not advisable for artistic decorations. By keeping it well closed in the vials, it will stay moist for years. Many pieces have been spoiled by the bad handling of this article, being applied too generously and causing it to run over the decorations. Use it from the vial direct on the china, but rub down your brush on the edge of the vial so as not to have too much liquid on it. It is not the gold that runs, it is the unnecessary quantity. Do not apply it near wet colors, as it will spread into them.

We give several hints on this article in the gold chapter. There is also a liquid burnish gold, made on the same principle as the above one, but containing more pure gold. This latter will fire matt and in burnishing will have the appearance of the Roman or unfluxed gold. There is also a special paste to be mixed with the liquid bright gold for the purpose of producing a

Roman gold effect. What we have seen of this article, does not give satisfactory results. Its color looks greenish and unnatural, becoming blackish with time. A recipe for liquid bright gold will be of interest to the student: Take sixteen grammes of gold metal, sixty-four grammes of nitric acid and sixty-four grammes of muriatic acid and place in a lukewarm place until thoroughly dissolved. Now place one-fourth gramme of zinc and one-fourth gramme of antimonchloride in the former solution and when everything is well amalgamated thin with 250 grammes of water.

In another jar put eight grammes of sulphur in powder, eight grammes of Venetian turpentine and forty grammes of thick oil of turpentine. Put in a lukewarm place and you will have a brownish, thick oil. Thin it now with twenty-five grammes of oil of lavender to keep the sulphur from separating. In this warm liquid pour your gold solution (also warm) and stir up continually, so that the gold will assimilate with the liquid (which, when cold, will be a thick heavy mass). Throw away, carefully, all the acids gathered on top, wash with warm water several times, throwing it away, again and again, and finely drip out all the water to the last drop. Put in this thirty-three grammes of oil of lavender, fifty grammes of flat oil of turpentine and warm the whole until everything is well amalgamated, and when cold should be ready for use. Should it be too thin, some time allowed for evaporating will bring it to the proper consistency.

CHAPTER LIV
GOLD MAKING RECIPE NO. 2.

This is another method of dissolving gold for the use of china and glass painting. Take five dwt. of gold ribbon, as thin as possible (gold coin is good but takes longer to dissolve). Place the gold in an open-mouthed jar with three ounces of muriatic acid and three ounces of nitric acid. These two acids together are called acqua regia. Cover the jar with a piece of glass and leave undisturbed until the gold is all dissolved and the liquid looks yellow. This liquid is called gold chloride. The dissolution may take from twelve to twenty-four hours, according to temperature. If at the end of such a period, the gold is not completely dissolved add more of the acids until it has all disappeared. Now take about three-fourths pound of copperas powder and put in enough water to dissolve it, stirring well; pour your gold solution in a good sized bowl (preferable with spout) add to it one-half pint clear water, and in that pour half of the copperas saturate made previously. Strong fumes will quickly arise, and a dark brown substance will precipitate to the bottom of the bowl. Leave it alone for about two hours, then carefully pour the liquid out into another bowl, and put aside the brown deposit, which is the gold. On the liquid just taken out, pour more copperas, so as to precipitate any gold that may be left there. Later remove the liquid and collect the brown gold sediment, placing it with the first one. Having done the above work correctly, add one pint of very hot water into the brown gold sediment, and stir up with a glass rod. Allow it to settle, throw water carefully away, and rewash with more hot water three times. Now throw into the gold one ounce of muriatic acid it free it from any trace of iron sulphate left by the copperas, and wash three or more times with very hot water. The powder having settled at the bottom, throw the last water away and dry on a warm place. This powder is prepared with oil and flux as given on Page 40 of this book.

CHAPTER LV
Recipes.
GROUNDING OIL.

One pound proportion. Eight ounces of boiled linseed oil, five ounces essence of turpentine, and three ounces of asphaltum. Place the whole over a gas stove, being careful that the fire should not reach the oil and cause a blaze. Stir continually, allowing it to boil for one-half hour. For the stirring use a stick having a small bag of litharge at its end. Cool the oil and place in jar keeping it well closed.

VARNISH FOR ACID ETCHINGS.

Good etching asphalt for acid etching can be made as follows: Dissolve four ounces of Burgundy pitch in ten ounces of turpentine; then take two ounces of lamp black well ground with turpentine, mix well with two ounces of balsam of copaiba. Put the two mixtures together and keep in well closed vessel. When needed dilute with turpentine. Brunswick black, used for stove blacking, is also a good article for acid etching.

CHAPTER LVI

SILVER DEPOSIT.

Gold and silver deposits seen on fine glass or china vases, trays, etc. (Properly called silver plated glass), is done by placing such vases into an electro plating bath, having one polar wire connected with the pieces to be decorated, and the other wire attached to a plate of silver or gold, as the case may be. This electrical connection will deposit the metal on the vases, and the longer the bath, the thicker the coating.

IMITATION ETCHINGS.

CHAPTER LVII

This is an imitation etching with color and low relief. Paint a border design in ivory yellow matt. By border design we mean the scroll or flower composing the border. Use the matt color rather heavy, then fire. Over such a fired border apply bright gold, covering not only the matt design, but also the background from upper line to lower line closing in the border. In other words, apply an all-over coating of the liquid bright gold and fire. In the third firing cover the gold applied on the previous firing, with a coat of dark green lustre, or brilliant green lustre, and you will have a very pretty effect.

SECOND IMITATION ETCHING.

Another imitation etching can be made by painting scrolls, etc., with finely-broken and sifted china powder (that is the body with which the china is made). Add to this fine powder one-eighth flux and mix with water or oil. After the firing, cover the whole border with all-over gold and the painted parts will look relief and matt etched.

CHAPTER LVIII

STANDARD PRICE LIST FOR FIRING.

The following list is given here to acquaint students with standard prices (considered fair), for the firing of decorated china. The size of the pieces should be considered, so that when we give, for instance, "Tray," it is natural that a large tray should bring more than a medium or small size. In making up the following list, we have endeavored to have so much money returns for the firing of a full kiln of china. After all, when one considers that a bad firing will spoil the best decoration, we must be willing to pay a fair price to the decorator attending to this matter in the proper way:

It may be hinted at the fact that the firing, person cannot be held responsible for breakage in the firing, as accidents are always apt to happen to people handling the china. *Prices follow next page.*

PIECE	FIRING PRICE
Creamer	10-15
Sugar	10-15-20
Teapot	15-20-25
Chop Trays	25-30
Cake Plates	20-30
B. & C. Trays	15-20-35
Placques	40-50-60
Table Tops	40-50-75-$1.00
Tankards	50-85
Lemonade Pitcher	25-30-35
Claret Pitcher	30-40
Jardinieres	35-85-$1.10
Punch Bowls	45-55-60-$1.10
Celery Dish	25-30
Spoon Tray	10-15
Olive Dish	15
Vases	20-85-$1.10
Tete-a-Tete Tray	40-50
Cracker Jar	30-40
Tobacco Jar	35
Chocolate Pot	35
Fish, Meat, Platters	60-85-$1.25
Salad, Berry Bowls	20-30-50
Bonbonnieres	15-25-35
Cup and Saucer	15
Plates, each	10-15
Half doz. plates 30-60 1 doz. plates	50-$1.00

An additional price of 20 per cent for firing
Belleek, Satsumas or Soft Chinas.

CHAPTER LIX
AIR BRUSH DECORATIONS.

Large decorating establishments, glass factories, or potteries doing a very large number of china or glass pieces of the same "decoration," use the *air brush* for their ground-laying and tinting, covering the whole piece or a part of it. The air brush is made on the principle of the atomizer or sprayer, used for medical purposes. The color in powder is mixed with one part of *Venice-Turpentine* and six parts of spirits of turpentine; mixed well. This is absolutely essential, as this mixture must pass through the sprayer having a very small aperture, which can be easily clogged up. However, the air brush is used with *air pressure* taken from a special tank and worked by pedals or power. This air, pressed through the *receptacle* containing the color, will be so powerful that the color will come out finely pulverized and turning the spray on the china or glass to be decorated, will leave a beautiful coating, not easily matched by other processes. We have tried to explain the air brush in an easy way, but the student should realize that the article used with satisfactory results at those potteries is rather expensive and more complicated than a medical pulverizer. For instance, the air brush has an aperture that can be regulated in working, so that the decorator can not only make a broad spray, but can reduce it to a small spray the size of a pin point. He can turn this to any part of the china and even make scrolls and lines with it. By covering the china with a design cut out on oily paper, and an air brush spray of color passed over the whole piece of china, he will make a stencilling effect, as the paper will be afterward taken off, and the design will appear in clean, white china. Lustre colors make pretty effects with air brush decoration and even liquid gold and silver. The air brush made for decorating purposes, namely the receptacle for color and spray, can be purchased separately from the air tank. Beautiful, even grounds, seen on cheap crockery, are always made with the air brush, as this work goes quickly and is very satisfactory. On account of the fine color spray produced by the air brush, the shop where this work is done is furnished with an *air drawing* apparatus, which apparatus draws out of the window the surplus volatilized color in the air. This color would be very injurious to the lungs and stomach of the decorator.

CHAPTER LX

KILNS

Having been asked several times by students. on the possibility of building their own kilns, I was compelled to advise them not to undertake such a task with the purpose of saving money, as the building of such an article requires experimenting on the ways the fire is drawn in by the draft, and properly distributed around the box, on the thickness of the walls, so that fire can be accomplished within a limited time, and the kind of burner, draft, etc. All this costs money and time, and a good kiln bought would be very much cheaper than a bad home-made kiln. However, so as to give a fair idea of the construction, I will give here the following version written by me for the Chicago Daily News:

HOW TO BUILD A KILN

The construction of a kiln for firing decorated china, in a nutshell, is one pot inside the other with the fire running between them. The inside pot contains the china and is well closed to prevent the fire from entering and affecting the decorations, while the outside pot contains, or rather closes in, the fire and has an opening at the top or side for the chimney or any outlet for smoke and soot, and one at the bottom for the fire.

The space between the two pots for a general size kiln may be about two inches. The inside pot is lifted and supported at every corner, leaving space to allow free circulation of the fire.

The burner (gas or oil) is placed underneath the big pot—directly under the opening, and the draft from the chimney will draw the fire up around all sides of the inside pot.

If the opening of the kiln is at the side, a door can be worked in instead of the cover used for a top opening.

In order to provide an even heat in all parts of the kiln, have an extra heavy bottom, as this receives the fire direct and would otherwise heat up quickly, while the other parts would be half fired.

Having built several experimental kilns of iron or bricks, I find that the difficulty lies in producing an even firing at the different parts of the kiln. Brick kilns are good and are built on the same general principle, but the more modern kilns have the inside pot or straight box made of fibre tile and the outside pot or box of thick iron sheet. They are built on four legs and can be easily removed.

It may be a pleasure to build and use a kiln of your own make, but it will cost you more money than a kiln bought and guaranteed to be good.

Kiln pots made of iron will expand and contract with every firing and will quickly crack, necessitating continual repairing with fire clay, and will eventually allow fire or smoke to enter and damage the china.

The writer once made a kiln and for the two pots adopted two kitchen utensils, such as are used to boil water in, and had fair results

Present trend is to use electric kilns. They cost more but they are more easily handled. Write for prices.

Campana's Reliable Lustre Colors

	Per Bot		
Opal	$0.18	Dark Green	.35
Orange	.18	Transparent Green	.45
Warm Gray	.18	Turquoise Blue	.28
Yellow	.18	Blue Green	.45
Light Green	.18	Black (prices change)	1.50
White	.18	Rose	55
Shamy Brown	.18	Dark Blue	.55
Yellow Brown	.18	Iridescent (strong)	.60
Mother of Pearl	.24	Steel Blue	.60
Yellow Pearl	.28	Violet	.65
Green Pearl	.28	Purple	.70
Pigeon Gray Pearl	.28	Silver Lustre	2.50
Brilliant Green	.28	Copper Bronze	1.15
Olive Green	.28	Ruby	1.25
Blue Gray	.28	Essence for thinning	.18
		Brown Dk.	1.50

If you wish to apply a more even background with lustre colors, you may warm the china very lightly before the application, but do not warm too much. O trifle of lavender oil mixed with them will help also in producing even lustre grounds.

A black ground makes warm colors, such as red, orange, pinks, etc., look warmer, while the same black ground diminishes cold colors, such as blues, blue-greens, or yellows. A white background on the contrary, makes warm colors, such as reds, etc., look less bright, while the blues, yellows, etc., appear more brilliant. Gold is an excellent color to place between contrasting shades, the brilliant glimmer of the gold harmonizing and allowing the colors to appear to better advantage.

To make fine lines on flat round pieces such as plates, you may use a *compass liner*. The liner is the instrument always found on compass boxes, and has the two pointed tongs coming together at the end. The color, in nearly liquid form, is applied in between the tongs with a knife and lines drawn around as done with the pencil compass. To make the article steady, put a small piece of tape or glued paper in the center of the china plate.

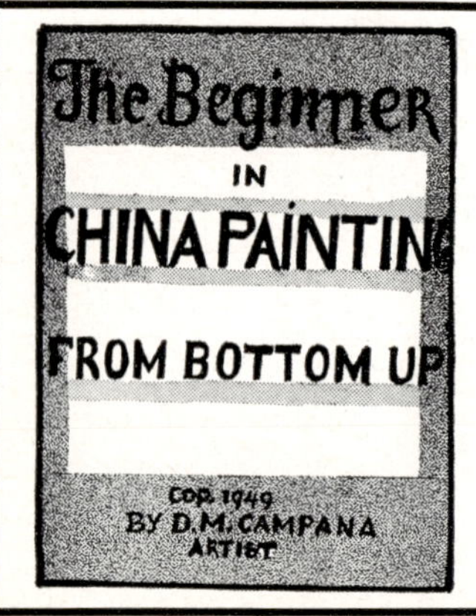

"THE BEGINNER IN CHINA PAINTING"

FOR

NEW STUDENTS

40c — Mail 5c

First Instructions

CERAMETTE FOR DECORATIVE PIECES, SIGNS, LIFE SIZE PORTRAITS— BEAUTIFUL, EVERLASTING

Ceramette, sister to china painting, is my next contribution to the field of ceramic art. Portrait from life looks brilliant, does not fade, will stand any temperature and is the latest. This work is handled as follows: Procure a slab of steel from enameling concerns. They have them coated with a coat of porcelain enamel, baked at 2000 degrees Fahrenheit. It comes to you with a beautiful white surface. You now plan your decorations which may be flower, landscape, or ornaments. I paint portraits natural size. The colors are the ceramic color used in china painting; they stand the same handling. They are baked like china and are as glazy and smooth. In this case you do large pieces, while china pieces are small. For interior decoration ceramette is great. Think of a two by three yard slab painted for interior decoration with any kind of decoration.

For advertising purposes there is a large field; lettering, figures, flowers, and any ornament, which can be outside in any weather element or inside as pictures.

I have a special booklet describing the whole system. Cost is 75c. Ask for Ceramette booklet.

These slabs can stand as much as ten firings and repainting without danger of hurting your work.

Use a long metal article to place your ceramette in the hot kiln and to take it out. Do this work fast so that you do not lose too much heat in the kiln. In this case you can leave your ceramette in the kiln two to three minutes instead of two.

TO CLOSE THIS BOOK

The present reprint of this book is the 10th. I might say that it is 50 years since I first published it, and it reminds me of my entry in the field of instructing ladies how to paint china, with Messrs. Bishop, Aulich and Campana in Chicago, in 1900. I give a version of my first exhibition at the Art Institute of Chicago, printed in the Chicago Tribune, as follows: "The yearly exhibit of ceramic opened yesterday at the Art Institute of Chicago. There are many good pieces and some which it is better not to mention. This year we have a new exhibitor, Mr. D. M. Campana, a real artist of the brush. His style is broad, his drawing is perfect, his technique the best we have seen.

"His Sighs of the Petals is a delicate poetic head of a nymph; his Diana (natural size) is a nude of a lady reclining, and a third is a decorative figure design full of color and verve. Two large flower pieces, roses and chrysanthemums, are treated with broad style and beautiful in decorative design, something we never saw before. The visitors of this exhibition were many and after having seen the whole exhibition they all returned to see Mr. Campana's exhibit. Mr. Campana was a student at the Academy of Fine Arts in Venice, Italy."

Mr. Campana was award three first prizes with gold medals in three traveling National Ceramic Exhibitions by 12 of our largest cities.

"I Strike the Happy Hours," by D. M. Campana

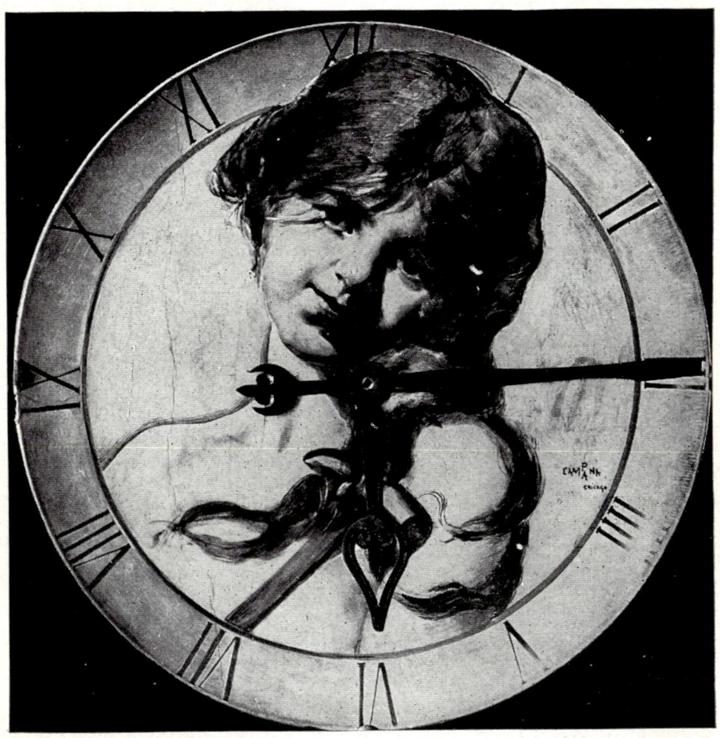

The above dial was painted with mineral colors on a 36-inch steel slab, coated with white porcelain and baked five times at 1500 degrees Fahrenheit. It was to be used in a high living room of a large mansion in a special built chime hall clock. The owner of the mansion posed for this picture painted by D. M. Campana.

The wide band where the hours are is in clear gold, the numbers are in black and the center of the dial was painted in gold and fired, to be covered with a coating of light green lustre with a very pretty effect. Her hair was ebony black.

ART PUBLICATIONS
All Written and Published by D. M. Campana, Artist
Chicago, Illinois

Popular, Useful and at Moderate Cost

Add 15c Each for Mailing.

The Teacher of Oil Paintings. By D. M. Campana.
Teaches the easiest method to learn oil painting. Landscape, figure, animal life, still life. A practical book. (13th Edition.) Price **85c.**

The Teacher of Water Color Painting. By D. M. Campana.
Teaching flowers, figure, landscape, etc., in a plain, clear manner. (Tenth edition.) Price **85c.**

The Teacher of Landscape Painting. By D. M. Campana.
(Seventh Edition.) Teaches how to start and finish a landscape, how to harmonize effects, colors, etc. Price **85c.**

The Teacher of Drawing. By D. M. Campana.
A book giving a systematic method of learning how to draw from nature. (Fifth Edition.) Price **$1.00.**

The Teacher of Figure Painting and Portraits. Fourth edition. By D. M. Campana. Teaches how to start and how to finish. Gives colors, methods, etc. Price **85c.**

Books of Monograms and Lettering. By D. M. Campana.
Contains a large variety of all styles (thousands of them). (Fourth Edition.) Price **85c.**

The Teacher of Pastel Painting. By D. M. Campana.
It teaches how to handle pastel pictures, how to start and how to finish them. Paper to use, quality of pastel, how to fasten them, etc. Price **85c.** (Fifth Edition.)

The Teacher of Geometrical Drawing. By D. M. Campana.
A book of instruction on geometry with very many illustrations and clearly taught. For schools or students. Price **85c.** (2nd Edition.)

The Teacher of Flower and Fruit Painting. By D. M. Campana.
This book explains individual colors to use in painting of flowers and fruit. A practical and useful book. Price **85c.** (Fourth Edition.)

The Teacher of Picture Frame Finishing. By D. M. Campana.
It teaches how to gild, how to burnish, how to apply gold leaf, how to make a frame, etc. Price **85c.** (3rd Edition.)

Art Drawing Made Easy. By D. M. Campana.
A system for beginners to learn the fundamental methods. An easy and practical way to learn drawing. 4th Ed. Price **85c.**

The Teacher of Animal Painting. By D. M. Campana.
It gives the colors to use for varied animals. It teaches the best way to paint them. Many illustrations. Price **85c.** (2nd Ed.)

Stained Glass Decorations Without Baking. By D. M. Campana.
Painted with Crystal Colors, beautiful windows and clear effects, very easily taught by this book. Price **85c.**

The Teacher of Photograph Painting. By D. M. Campana.
Teaches how to tint photographs both for art sake and for commercial purposes. Price **85c.** (3rd enlarged Edition.)

Book, "The Teacher of China Painting." By D. M. Campana.
A very complete text book for beginners and advanced workers. (Sixth Edition.) Price **85c.**

The Artist and Decorators. By D. M. Campana.
A large collection of high class decorations and artistic suggestions in all styles. A book for ambitious workers, such as decorators, designers, artists, engravers. About 500 ideas. Price **$2.50.**

Greeting Cards For All Occasions. Hundreds of them by D. M. Campana. Price **85c** (new).

Self-Taught Picture Painting. No. 3. By D. M. Campana.
With 10 Pictures in colors. Price **$1.25.** 4th reprint.

Anatomy and Human Form. By D. M. Campana. New. **85c.**

Mirror Making and Painting. By D. M. Campana.
Teaches varied decorations. Price **65c.**

Book—Roses and How to Paint Them. By D. M. Campana.
Teaching method for painting roses in water color, china, oil, silk and other branches. Given exclusively to roses with colored studies. (Fifth Edition.) Price **85c.**

The Teacher of Textile Painting. By D. M. Campana, 3rd Edition.
Teaches how to paint all kinds of cloth, silk, velvet, satin, cotton dresses, hats, tapestry, etc. Price **85c.**

The Teacher of Lamp Shade Making. By D. M. Campana.
Teaches how to build and decorate paper shades, silk shades, cotton shades, etc.—giving all details. Price **85c.**

The Teacher of Jesso Decorating. By D. M. Campana.
A booklet guiding you and explaining the best way to start and decorate plaques, book ends, candle sticks, etc. Price **85c.**

The Teacher of Linoleum Printing. By D. M. Campana.
It gives the best method and the correct way to make prints for schools or individuals, with illustrations. Price **65c.**

Enamel Decorations. By D. M. Campana.
On porcelain and glass—with illustrations. Teaches the safest enamels and colors. Describes cause for chipping off, etc. Price **85c.**

The Teacher of Lettering Show Cards and Sign Painting. By D. M. Campana. 85c. (Second Edition.)

Amateur Artist Encyclopedia.
Contains over 50 different branches of art and craft. By D. M. Campana. Price **85c.** 3rd edition.

Book of 1000 Decorations and Ideas. By D. M. Campana.
A variety of conventionalized subjects from nature for all kinds of decorations. A very popular book. Price **85c.** 2nd Ed.

The Teacher of Casting, Modeling, Sculpturing, Woodcarving and Pottery. By D. M. Campana. Price **85c.** 2nd Edition.

Book of Decorative Designs. No. 1. By D. M. Campana.
Full of pretty borders and ideas for all kinds of decorations. (Third Edition.) Price **90c.**

Book of Decorative Designs. No. 2. By D. M. Campana.
Contains 191 complete designs of all shapes and styles. (Third Edition. Price **90c.**

Book on Leather Craft. By D. M. Campana. 3rd Edition.
Explaining tooling, carving, painting, polishing, etc. Illustrated with many patterns for bags, etc. Price **85c.**

Book of Decorative Designs. No. 4.
An entirely different collection of decorative ideas, original and pretty. Price **90c.**

Historical Ornaments and the Teacher of Designing. By D. M. Campana. Book No. 5.
A fine collection of Historical Ornaments. Also teaches how to learn designing. Price **$1.00.**

Interior Decorations. By D. M. Campana. Book No. 6.
Full of pretty suggestions for interior decorations. Price **90c.**

Designs and Patterns for China and Glass Decorations. By D. M. Campana. Book No. 7. ((3rd Edition.)
A large variety of ideas, good for all kinds of work and craft. Price **$1.00.**

Book—100 Lustre Color Combinations. By D. M. Campana.
How to make them, with all the latest effects. (Second Edition.) Price **85c.** For china and glass.

Book on Firing Porcelain and Glass. By D. M. Campana.
With directions for stacking, repairing, etc. (Third Edition.) Price **85c.**

Acid Etchings. By D. M. Campana.
On porcelain and glass—with illustrations. Describes from beginning to end the whole process of etching in on china and glass. Price **85c.**

Figurines Made at Home. By D. M. Campana.
Teaches the making and painting. Price **85c.**

Glass Decorations and Firing. By D. M. Campana.
A booklet teaching how to decorate and fire crystal glass. Such method can be followed with any quality of glass. Price **55c.**

Ceramic Photography. By D. M. Campana. 2nd edition.
Gives recipes and methods for making photographs on china and enamels. Price **85c.**

Book of Designs and Color Schemes. By D. M. Campana.
A publication in colors, complete; 120 pages of designs in colors and directions. Better than 6 months' lessons. Price **$10.00.** (For china decorations.)

Studies in Series. (20 Series.) By D. M. Campana.
Each series contains 6 designs in colors with many directions. Flowers, fruit, conventional. Each series **75c.**

Teacher of Batik Painting.
Comprising a variety of textile materials. With full instructions. Price **85c;** mail, **5c.**

Campana's Gold Paint Formula. How to Make It. For Porcelain and Glass. By D. M. Campana.
In paste form to be baked. A valuable secret recipe. **$10.00.**

Art Anatomy and Human Form. By. D. M. Campana.
Finely illustrated. **85c,** mail **10c.**

Teacher of Pottery Made at Home. (New)   By D. M. Campana.
Price **85c.**

Teacher of Ceramette Painting. By D. M. Campana.
Steel slab coated with enamel and baked at 2000° F. Painted over with mineral colors and baked at 1500° F. Decorations are everlasting. Something new. Instructions. Price **75c.**

Teacher of Commercial Advertising. By D. M. Campana.
A how you do book, in a big field. Price **85c.**

Beginner of China Painting. **35c;** mail **5c.**

Beginner of Oil Painting. **35c;** mail **5c.**

Beginner of Water Color Painting. **35c;** mail **5c.**

NOTICE—The above publications by D. M. Campana are sold at the stores selling artists' materials and art literature.

These books are sold at low prices, contain much useful information on the varied branches of art and are as instructive as any book costing several dollars. If you can't find the wanted book in your store, write the author of this book, D. M. Campana, Artist, Chicago 10, Illinois enclosing the amount specified and you will receive it promptly. **Add 15c for mailing.**

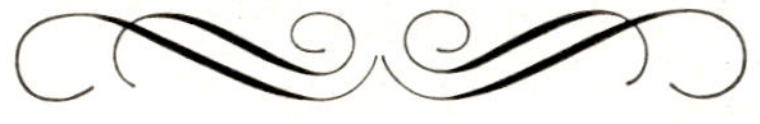

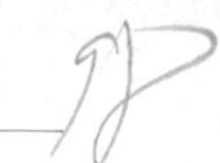

C.... ....COLORS

For Ch......   ....nooth, Glossy,
                             ....pana's.

YELLOW
Trenton Iv....
Imperial Ivc....
Ivory yello....
Neutral yell....
Primrose ye....
Deep yellow orange............ .15
Egg yellow........................ .15
Lemon yellow (rich).......... .15
Albert yello.... 15
Canary ....

RO.... AND PINKS
Sweet Pea, pink..................**$0.20**
Rose color, best.................. .30
Rose salmon...................... .20
Pe.... lossoms.................... .35
A.... .... beauty.................. .40

GREENS
V.... reen (light)............**$0.15**
O.... ....een........................ .15
Br.... ....reen.................... .15
Sh.... .... green.................. .15
Pea.... .... green................ .15
Pers.... .... green................ .15
Gray .... green.................. .15
Sulta.... green (rich)............ .15
Russ.... n green.................. .15
Empi.... e green.................. .15
Myrtle green...................... .15
Moss green...................... .15
Roy.... l green.................... .15
App.... green.................... .15
Ne.... green...................... .15
Dee.... blue green................ .15
Yellow green.................... .15
Sha.... ing green................ .15
Darkest green.................... .15

BROWNS
Yellow brown....................**$0.15**
Chestnut brown.................. .15
Meissen brown.................. .15
Dee.... red brown................ .15
I.... ....ing brown.................. .30
.... brown.................... .15
.... n brown.................. .25
.... orown.................... .25

REDS
Po.... padour red (light)...... .30
P.... .... v red...................... .35
.... (No. 2)................ .13

.... (No. 2)............	$0.30
.... d (dark)......	.30
	.15
	.35
	.30

.... LUES
Sevres blue......................**$0.15**
Turquoise blue.................. .15
Baby blue........................ .15
Con.... ....h.... ....lue.... .... .15
.... .30
Air blue.......................... .30
Royal blue........................ .30
Aztec blue........................ .30
Banding blue.................... .20

FLESH TINTS
Flesh, soft tint..................**$0.40**
Flesh, shadow.................... .40
Flesh, dark shadow............ .40
Flesh, gray...................... .40
Flesh, transparency............ .40
Hair black........................ .40

GRAYS
Satzuma tint....................**$0.15**
Warm gray........................ .15
Gray for flowers................ .15
Royal Copenhagen gray.... .20
Flesh gray........................ .25
Pearl gray........................ .15
Ashes of roses.................. .25

BLACKS
Best black......................**$0.15**
Outlining black.................. .15
Purple black...................... .35
Hair black........................ .35

VIOLETS
Violet color No. 2.... ....**$0.35**
Violet color...................... .45
Violet of iron No. 2............ .15
Violet of iron.................... .20
Deep violet of gold............ .45
Light violet of gold............ .40

GLAZES AND FLUXES
Flux, soft or hard............**$0.15**
Ivory glaze, for dusting.... .15

PURPLES AND RUBIES
Royal purple....................**$0.40**
Crimson purple.................. .60
Ruby purple, brilliant........ .60
Ruby purple, No. 2.......... .. .55

Campana's Golds — Roman and Unfluxed Gold   Ask for Price.

Campana's Golds — Liquid Bright Gold. Ask for Prices

My Roman Gold has been now perfected like the

old Hasburg's Gold. Ask for Price.

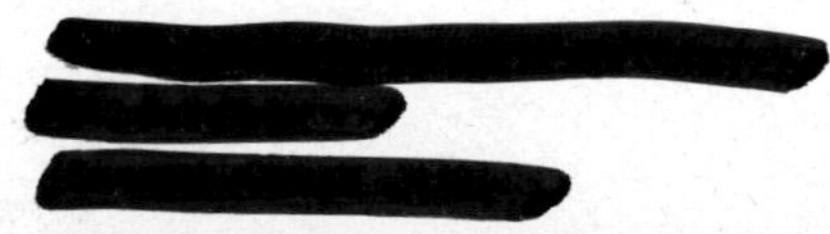